THE FATHERS OF THE CHURCH

A NEW TRANSLATION

VOLUME 119

THE FATHERS OF THE CHURCH

A NEW TRANSLATION

EDITORIAL BOARD

Thomas P. Halton
The Catholic University of America
Editorial Director

Elizabeth Clark
Duke University

Robert D. Sider
Dickinson College

Joseph T. Lienhard, S.J.
Fordham University

Michael Slusser
Duquesne University

David G. Hunter
University of Kentucky

Cynthia White
University of Arizona

Kathleen McVey
Princeton Theological Seminary

Rebecca Lyman
Church Divinity School
of the Pacific

David J. McGonagle
Director
The Catholic University of America Press

FORMER EDITORIAL DIRECTORS
Ludwig Schopp, Roy J. Deferrari, Bernard M. Peebles,
Hermigild Dressler, O.F.M.

Carole Monica C. Burnett
Staff Editor

ORIGEN

HOMILIES ON JUDGES

Translated by
ELIZABETH ANN DIVELY LAURO

THE CATHOLIC UNIVERSITY OF AMERICA PRESS
Washington, D.C.

Copyright @ 2010
THE CATHOLIC UNIVERSITY OF AMERICA PRESS
All rights reserved
Printed in the United States of America

The paper used in this publication meets the minimum
requirements of the American National Standards for
Information Science—Permanence of Paper for Printed
Library Materials, ANSI z39.48—1984.
∞

LIBRARY OF CONGRESS CATALOGING-IN-PUBLICATION DATA
Origen.
[Homélies sur les Juges. English]
Homilies on Judges / Origen ; translated by
Elizabeth Ann Dively Lauro.
p. cm. — (The fathers of the church :
a new translation ; v. 119)
Includes bibliographical references and indexes.
ISBN 978-0-8132-0119-1 (cloth : alk. paper)
ISBN 978-0-8132-2773-3 (pbk.)
1. Bible. O.T. Judges—Sermons—Early works to 1800. 2.
Sermons, Latin—Translations into English. I. Dively Lauro,
Elizabeth.
II. Title.   III. Series.
BS1305.54.O7513 2010
222'.3206—dc22
2009014298

CONTENTS

Acknowledgments	ix
Abbreviations	xi
Select Bibliography	xiii

Introduction — 1

HOMILIES ON JUDGES

Homily One	39
Homily Two	51
Homily Three	61
Homily Four	70
Homily Five	76
Homily Six	84
Homily Seven	94
Homily Eight	100
Homily Nine	111

INDICES

General Index	121
Index of Holy Scripture	135

ACKNOWLEDGMENTS

I wish to thank my faithful mentors and friends, John C. Cavadini and Brian E. Daley, for their encouragement in this present endeavor. I am grateful also to Carole Monica Burnett, the anonymous readers, and all the staff involved with the Fathers of the Church series at the Catholic University of America Press for this opportunity and for their assistance and support. I also wish to acknowledge the constant help of my in-laws Marie and Lawrence Lauro, the patience of my daughter Sofia, and the insightful editorial input of my husband Lino along the way.

ABBREVIATIONS

Primary Works
Hist. eccl.   Eusebius, *Ecclesiastical History*

Editions, Translations, Series, and Journals
ACW   Ancient Christian Writers Series
FOTC   Fathers of the Church Series
JTS   *Journal of Theological Studies*
LXX   Septuagint
NPNF2   Nicene and Post-Nicene Fathers, Second Series
RSR   *Recherches de sciences religieuses*
RSV   Revised Standard Version of Bible
SC   Sources Chrétiennes
SPCK   Society for Promoting Christian Knowledge, London
TU   Texte und Untersuchungen

In dedication to my husband Lino

and

*In memory of my father
Robert Roy Dively (1935–2006)*

SELECT BIBLIOGRAPHY

Baehrens, W. *Überlieferung und Textgeschichte der lateinischen erhaltenen Origenes Homilien zum Alten Testament.* Texte und Untersuchungen, vol. 42.1. Leipzig, 1916.

Balthasar, Hans Urs von. *Origen, Spirit and Fire: A Thematic Anthology of His Writings.* Trans. Robert J. Daly. Washington, DC: The Catholic University of America Press, 1984. Reprint, 2001.

Crouzel, Henri. *Origen: The Life and Thought of the First Great Theologian.* Trans. A. S. Worrell. Edinburgh: T&T Clark, 1989.

Daniélou, Jean. *Origen.* Trans. Walter Mitchell. New York: Sheed and Ward, 1955.

Dively Lauro, Elizabeth Ann. *The Soul and Spirit of Scripture within Origen's Exegesis.* Boston and Leiden: Brill Academic Publishers, Inc., 2005.

Greer, Rowan A., trans. *Origen: An Exhortation to Martyrdom, Prayer and Selected Works.* New York: Paulist, 1979.

Heine, Ronald E., trans. "Introduction." *Origen: Homilies on Genesis and Exodus.* Fathers of the Church 71. Washington, DC: The Catholic University of America Press, 1982.

Lubac, Henri de. *Histoire et Esprit: L'Intelligence de l'Écriture d'après Origène.* Théologie 16. Paris: Aubier, 1950.

———. "'Typologie' et 'Allégorisme.'" *Recherches de sciences religieuses* 34 (1947): 180–226.

McGuckin, John Anthony, ed. *The Westminster Handbook to Origen.* Louisville and London: Westminster John Knox Press, 2004.

———. *The Westminster Handbook to Patristic Theology.* Louisville and London: Westminster John Knox Press, 2004.

Messié, Pierre, Louis Neyrand, and Marcel Borret, eds. and trans. *Origène: Homélies sur les Juges.* Paris: Les Éditions du Cerf, 1993.

Moser, Maureen Beyer. *Teacher of Holiness: The Holy Spirit in Origen's Commentary on the Epistle to the Romans.* Gorgias Dissertations 17. Early Christian Studies 4. Piscataway, NJ: Gorgias Press, 2005.

Murphy, Francis X. *Rufinus of Aquileia (345–411): His Life and Works.* Washington, DC: The Catholic University of America Press, 1945.

Nautin, Pierre. *Origène: sa vie et son oeuvre*. Christianisme antique 1. Paris: Beauchesne, 1977.

Torjesen, Karen Jo. *Hermeneutical Procedure and Theological Method in Origen's Exegesis*. Patristische Texte und Studien 28. Berlin: De Gruyter, 1986.

Wagner, M. *Rufinus the Translator: A Study of his Theory and Practice as Illustrated in his Version of the Apologetica of S. Gregory Nazianzen*. Washington, DC: The Catholic University of America Press, 1945.

INTRODUCTION

INTRODUCTION

Apart from Augustine of Hippo and Thomas Aquinas, there is no father of the Christian Church who has so comprehensively influenced its theology, scriptural exegesis, and practice as Origen of Alexandria (c. 185–254 A.D.).[1] Unlike his giant counterparts, Origen has elicited deep hatred as well as fierce devotion from the time of his death to the present. Though Origen was officially declared a heretic three times before the seventh century,[2] Christian theologians have read him throughout the centuries and often explicitly relied upon his thought.[3] In the 1800s, scholars began to disregard taboos associated with Origen and started creating modern editions and translations of his works. Both theologians and Church leaders now recognize Origen as a master of the spiritual life,[4] much as did the early

1. As a preconciliar theologian and extensive exegete of Scripture, Origen helped to pave the way, with regard both to terminology and ideas, for the early Church councils that would follow, including the Council of Nicaea (325), which formulated the first official statement of faith on the Trinity, and the Council of Chalcedon (431), which formulated the first official statement on Jesus Christ's humanity and divinity.

2. For the early disagreements over the orthodoxy of Origen's very influential works and his condemnations, see E. M. Harding, "Origenist Crises," *The Westminster Handbook to Origen*, ed. John Anthony McGuckin (Louisville and London: Westminster John Knox Press, 2004), 162–67. See also Joseph W. Trigg, *Origen*, The Early Christian Fathers (London and New York: Routledge, 1998), 62–66.

3. To name a few, Thomas Aquinas, Erasmus, and Meister Eckhart utilized the theology of Origen in their own works. We also know that Martin Luther read Origen's works (since Luther condemned Origen's exegetical method).

4. Very recently, Pope Benedict XVI (formerly Cardinal Joseph Ratzinger) made two speeches to audiences at the Vatican in Rome praising Origen's legacy for the Church. In the first speech, delivered April 25, 2007, the Pope referred to Origen as "one of the greatest teachers of the Christian faith" because of his combination of scholarship, preaching, teaching, and "exempla-

desert monks of the fourth and fifth centuries and the heirs of their legacies.[5]

As we might expect from such a master, Origen's biblical commentaries, homilies, and treatises navigate his audience through the challenging terrain of spiritual growth.[6] His nine homilies on the book of Judges exemplify the theological principle that, for Origen, underlies spiritual growth: the human soul's struggle to fight off vices and grow in the virtues, which are Christ.[7]

The nine homilies on Judges interpret texts of chapters 2 to 7 of that book. In them, Israel, before the age of kings but after the death of Joshua (that is, Jesus son of Nun,[8] the great succes-

---

ry moral conduct." In a second speech, delivered on May 2, 2007, the Pope praised Origen for his teachings on prayer and the Church, especially his dedication to and promotion of *lectio divina*.

5. Rowan A. Greer mentions that Origen's theology was the basis for "an ideology of monasticism ... developed by the Cappadocians" and "carried forward" by men such as "Evagrius Ponticus, the pseudo-Dionysius, John Cassian, Gregory the Great, Maximus the Confessor, and others." See Rowan A. Greer, *Origen: An Exhortation to Martyrdom, Prayer and Selected Works*, The Classics of Western Spirituality (New York: Paulist Press, 1979), 34. Similarly, Jean Daniélou lists the following leaders of the ascetical Christian life as directly influenced by Origen: the Cappadocians, Eusebius of Caesarea, Jerome, John Cassian, Evagrius Ponticus, Hilary of Poitiers, and Ambrose of Milan. See Jean Daniélou, *Origen*, trans. Walter Mitchell (London and New York: Sheed and Ward, 1955), vii–viii. See also Hans Urs von Balthasar, ed., *Origen, Spirit and Fire: A Thematic Anthology of His Writings*, trans. Robert J. Daly (Washington, DC: The Catholic University of America Press, 1984; reprinted, 2001), Introduction, 1–3. Origen's theological and exegetical efforts definitely influenced, among other things, both early and contemporary monastic practices of *lectio divina*.

6. See Elizabeth Ann Dively Lauro, *The Soul and Spirit of Scripture Within Origen's Exegesis*, The Bible in Ancient Christianity 3 (Boston and Leiden: Brill Academic Publishers, Inc., 2005).

7. For Origen's idea that the virtues are to be identified with Christ himself, see *Comm in Song* 1.5 and commentary of this text in Dively Lauro, *The Soul and Spirit of Scripture*, 229–31, as well as *Hom in Jgs* 1.3.

8. This translation of the homilies employs "Jesus" in English for Joshua son of Nun as well as for Jesus Christ, since "Jesus" is equivalent to the Hebrew name Joshua, and Rufinus employs it in the Latin for both figures. Also, "Jesus" captures Origen's portrayal of Joshua as a type of Jesus Christ. Barbara J. Bruce chose the same practice in her translation of the homilies on Joshua. See *Origen: Homilies on Joshua*, Barbara J. Bruce, trans., and Cynthia White,

INTRODUCTION 5

sor to Moses), cyclically sins against God, consequently falls into the hands of enemies and suffers devastation and enslavement, eventually cries out to God for help, and, as a result, receives a judge sent by God to save them from their bondage. After periods of enjoying God's blessings, the Israelites invariably turn their backs on God and sin, thus repeating the cycle of enslavement, repentance, and salvation again. This cycle (a well-known motif in the Hebrew Scriptures) provides Origen a rich mine from which to unearth Scripture's call for his own audience to repent of their sins, cry out to God for help, and await God's salvific measures to bring them out of their personally chosen enslavements to sin.

This introduction addresses four matters that may assist in reading Origen's homilies on Judges. First, we consider the extant texts used for this translation. Since the original Greek of Origen's delivery is no longer extant, we explore the substantial evidence that favors the reliability of Rufinus of Aquileia's available Latin translation of these homilies. Second, we reflect on the possible dating of his delivery of these homilies as well as his likely audience. Third, we consider Origen's method of scriptural interpretation in order to clarify how he draws spiritual direction out of the biblical text. Fourth, we review the major theological themes, or spiritual lessons, that he draws from his exegesis of Judges. At the end, we describe the Latin edition used and the methods employed in translating it into English.

RUFINUS OF AQUILEIA'S TRANSLATION OF THE HOMILIES

The original Greek texts for Origen's nine homilies on Judges are no longer extant, but they survive in the Latin translation of Rufinus of Aquileia (341–411). Rufinus translated them from the original Greek into the Latin of his day, between approximately 401 and 403 A.D.[9] By his own account, Rufinus translat-

---

ed., FOTC 105 (Washington, DC: The Catholic University of America Press, 2002), 24 n. 4.

9. See Ronald E. Heine, trans., *Origen: Homilies on Genesis and Exodus*, FOTC 71 (Washington, DC: The Catholic University of America Press, 1982), 29. Heine

ed Origen's homilies at the request of friends for the edification of western Christians of his day,[10] that is, to provide spiritual direction to his own Latin audiences;[11] and his method of translating was likely determined by this end.[12]

To date, the definitive, collective statement on Rufinus's reliability and method in translating Origen remains that of Ronald E. Heine, who summarizes and assesses Rufinus's own prefaces and epilogues to his translations of Origen's works, taking into account also prior scholarship.[13] While, Heine points out, some

---

dates Rufinus's translation of the homilies on Judges during the same time period as those on Joshua. He determines that Rufinus translated them between 401 and 403 by considering (from cross-references in Rufinus's prefaces) the order in which Rufinus translated Origen's works within the broader timeframe of the years 397–411. Heine relies generally on Francis X. Murphy's placement of all of Rufinus's translations of Origen's works during this timeframe. See Heine, FOTC 71:28 n. 143, referring to Francis X. Murphy, *Rufinus of Aquileia (345–411): His Life and Works* (Washington, DC: The Catholic University of America Press, 1945). Heine informs us that C. Hammond, though having given different years for some specific works, also places all of Rufinus's translations of Origen's works within the same range of years: from 397 to 411. See Heine, FOTC 71:28 n. 144, citing C. Hammond, "The Last Ten Years of Rufinus' Life and the Date of his Move South from Aquileia," *JTS* (1977): 372–429, esp. 428–29.

10. See Bruce, trans., FOTC 105:15 n. 56, citing the prologue to Pamphilus, *Apology for Origen*, and the prologue to *The Recognitions of Clement*, and n. 58, citing the prologue to Origen, *Homilies on the Psalms*, and the prologue to Origen, *Homilies on Numbers*.

11. Heine cites Monica Wagner as concluding, after studying Rufinus's prefaces to his translations of Origen's works, that his purpose was "the moral advancement of his readers and this aim determined his method." See Heine, trans., FOTC 71:32 and 32 n. 166, quoting Monica Wagner, *Rufinus the Translator: A Study of his Theory and Practice as Illustrated in his Version of the Apologetica of S. Gregory Nazianzen*, (Washington, DC: The Catholic University of America Press, 1945), 11. Heine also cites Wagner as arguing that whatever changes Rufinus made to the text of Origen were done to make the text more intelligible and accessible to his own western, Latin audience. See Heine, trans., FOTC 71:32 nn. 166 and 167, citing Wagner, *Rufinus the Translator*, 11, and also citing as in general agreement Murphy, *Rufinus of Aquileia*, 227.

12. Bruce agrees with Wagner, Murphy, and Heine that Rufinus's purpose and audience helped to shape his method for translating Origen's works into Latin. See Bruce, trans., FOTC 105:15.

13. See Heine, trans., FOTC 71:27–39.

INTRODUCTION   7

scholars have dismissed Rufinus as an unreliable translator,[14] other scholars (generally more recent) disagree.

Scholars who closely analyze Rufinus's Latin translations with the available Greek show that Rufinus, though admittedly not a literal, word-for-word translator, proves reliable for Origen's ideas and thought if not his exact expression.[15] In particular, Henry Chadwick compared Rufinus's translation of *Comm in Rom* with Greek fragments found at Tura and concluded: "The voice is the voice of Origen, even though the hands are the hands of Rufinus."[16] In addition, J. Armitage Robinson com-

14. Heine, FOTC 71:30. Heine lists the following scholars as skeptical of Rufinus's translations and some of them, especially Eugène de Faye, as insistent on analyzing Origen's thought based only on what is extant in the original Greek: Hal Koch, *Pronoia und Paideusis* (Berlin: Walter de Gruyter & Co., 1932), 322f.; Eugène de Faye, *Origen and His Work*, trans. Fred Rothwell (London: Allen & Unwin, 1926), referred to by Koch, *Pronoia*, 323; G. W. Butterworth, *Origen: On First Principles* (New York: Harper and Row, 1966), xlvii; and Hanson, *Tradition*, 47; J. E. L. Oulton, "Rufinus' Translation of the Church History of Eusebius," *JTS* 30 (1929): 150. Also, Heinrich Hoppe finds that Rufinus misunderstands the Greek at times through a lack of carefulness, and changes theological and even rhetorical points at times, in "Rufin als Uebersetzer," *Studi dedicati alla memoria di Paola Ubaldi* (Milan, 1937), 142–49. In addition, Basil Studer argues that Rufinus and Jerome deliberately changed "Christological titles in Origen's works" in order to make his thought fit "the theology of their time," in "A propos des traductions d'Origène par Jérôme et Rufin," *Vetera Christianorum* 5 (1968): 137–55.

15. Heine, FOTC 71:30–33. In addition to the scholarship that follows in the text, Heine highlights the following scholarly support for Rufinus's translations: Manlio Simonetti favors Rufinus's translation sometimes over the Greek edition by Koetschau of *De principiis*. See Hanson's review of Simonetti's *I Principe di Origene*, Classici delle Religioni 4 (Turin: Unione Tipografico Editrice Torinese, 1968), in *JTS* n.s. 31 (1970): 181. Gustave Bardy finds Rufinus faithful to Origen's thought if not his exact expression, in *Recherches sur l'histoire du texte et des versions latines du* De Principiis *d'Origène* (Paris: Edouard Champion, 1923), 118–20. Walther Völker was comfortable enough with Rufinus's translation to base analyses of Origen's thought on the exact wording of the translations, in *Das Vollkommenheitsideal des Origenes* (Tübingen: J. C. B. Mohr, 1930), 17–18. Pierre Nautin finds Rufinus's translation of Pamphilus's *Apology for Origen* "almost literal" except with regard to "the discussion of the Trinity," in Pierre Nautin, *Origène: Sa vie et son oeuvre* (Paris: Beauchesne, 1977), 150–52.

16. Henry Chadwick rehabilitates the credibility of Rufinus's translation of

pared all the Greek in the Philocalia with the corresponding Latin translated by Rufinus and found that, while Rufinus's translation was paraphrastic, he had not changed much.[17] Henri Crouzel agrees, stating:

> [O]n the whole these are not literal translations, even when they set out to be such, but have been composed as independent literary works for the Latin public: paraphrases rather than translations. However, apart from omissions, *they render the ideas closely enough*. But, compared with the originals, they also reflect the difference of outlook between a Greek of the persecuted minority Church of the 3rd century and Latins of the triumphant Church of the end of the 4th.[18]

While, Crouzel points out, Rufinus translated with a different audience in mind from that of Origen or Origen's transcribers, still his translations are faithful to Origen's ideas. Crouzel also supports the view of Henri de Lubac, which launched the current deference toward using Rufinus's translations in studying Origen's thought:

> In this case more than in others, the right procedure is not to omit but to make use of on a massive scale. To have any chance of getting at the authentic Origen, there must be a multiplicity of quotations. Then parallel passages are a check on each other; they show each other's meaning and comment on it, especially when we look, for example, at a sentence in the Latin of Rufinus, another in the Latin of Jerome [a contemporary of Rufinus], and a third preserved in the original. Now it is not rare to be able to do that, and *from these comparisons an impression of unity emerges*.[19]

Comm in Rom against translator J. Scherer's accusation that Rufinus interpolated the text in places, in "Rufinus and the Tura Papyrus of Origen's Commentary on Romans," *JTS* n.s. 10 (1959): 19–37, esp. 25, quoted by Heine, FOTC 71:38–39.

17. J. Armitage Robinson, *The Philocalia of Origen* (Cambridge: Cambridge University Press, 1893), xxiv, cited by Bruce, FOTC 105:16.

18. Henri Crouzel, *Origen: The Life and Thought of the First Great Theologian*, trans. A. S. Worrall (San Francisco: Harper & Row, Publishers, 1989; originally, Paris: Pierre Zech Editeur, 1985), 42. Emphasis added.

19. Henri de Lubac, *Histoire et Esprit: L'Intelligence de l'Écriture d'après Origène* (Paris: Aubier Éditions Montaigne, 1950), 42, quoted by Crouzel, *Origen*, 48–49. Emphasis added.

INTRODUCTION 9

From a studied comparison of the parallel Greek and Latin texts available, then, scholarship tends to support the reliability of Rufinus as a translator.

Even where parallel Greek texts are not available, other scholars who have extensively studied Rufinus have proclaimed his general reliability as a translator. And, of course, most of the extant homilies by Origen survive only in Rufinus's Latin, with no parallel Greek text or Latin translation by Jerome. After analyzing Rufinus's motives and method of translation in the prefaces to his translations, Monica Wagner concluded that his paraphrasing and changes justifiably serve his purpose of rendering Origen to his fourth-century Latin audience more briefly and more clearly, without finding that he was unfaithful to Origen's meaning.[20] Francis X. Murphy is in agreement with Wagner on this point.[21] This general view directs the scholarship of Origen today, with theologians relying on Rufinus's translation for close textual analyses of Origen's writings in order to understand better the contribution of his exegesis and theology to Christian thought.

Although scholars today generally support the reliability of Rufinus's translation for studies of Origen's thought, it is useful to bear in mind the components of Rufinus's self-proclaimed method of translation. First, Rufinus claims that he follows Jerome's method of "translat[ing] the sense into Latin, and not word-for-word."[22] Second, Rufinus adds thoughts from Origen's other works to those places that he judged to have been interpolated by heretics, especially contradictions regarding the Trinity that did not seem to him to be characteristic of Origen.[23] Third, Rufinus also adds thoughts expressed elsewhere in Origen's

20. Wagner, *Rufinus the Translator*, 11, cited by Heine, FOTC 71:32 n. 166.
21. See Murphy, *Rufinus of Aquileia*, 227, cited by Heine, FOTC 71:32 n. 167.
22. Rufinus, *Apology against Jerome*, 2.40, quoted by Heine, FOTC 71:35 nn. 182 and 183 (cf. Jerome, *Epistle* 57.5) and cited by Bruce, FOTC 105:15 n. 60. Heine also cites for this point *Apology to Pope Anastasius* 7 and *Preface to the Letter of Gaudentius*.
23. Rufinus, *On the Adulteration of Origen's Writings, Preface to Heraclius in Ex-*

works whenever he thinks that his fourth-century Latin audience will otherwise find Origen unclear.[24] Fourth, Rufinus takes it upon himself to abbreviate Origen's text,[25] especially since, as

planation of Origen on the Letter of Paul to the Romans, Preface to De Principiis, 1.3, 3 and 1.2, and *Apology to Pope Anastasius* 7, cited by Heine, FOTC 71:33–35 nn. 170–78. Heine tells us more specifically that Rufinus thought he found conspicuous contradictions on three topics within Origen's works: "the Holy Spirit, on whether the Father and the Son are of one substance, and on the resurrection of the flesh," and that Origen would not have produced such glaring contradictions without comment. Moreover, Rufinus found a letter by Origen in which Origen himself complained of enemies changing his works. In addition, Rufinus was aware that the works of other theologians, for example, Hilary, Cyprian, and Damasus, had been changed by persons of questionable orthodoxy. Heine also points out that Rufinus would have been familiar with the body of Origen's works, including texts no longer extant. Therefore, Rufinus felt justified in identifying and correcting parts of Origen's works where he believed persons opposed to orthodoxy had altered them. For Rufinus's admission that he found texts altered as well as missing and that he added Origen's thoughts from other places within his works in order to create "continuity" within the Latin text, see *Preface to Comm in Rom*, 2, in *Origen: Commentary on the Epistle to the Romans, Books 1–5*, trans. Thomas P. Scheck, FOTC 103, vol. 1 of 2 vols. (Washington, DC: The Catholic University of America Press, 2001), 51. See also Crouzel, *Origen*, 46–47, for his judgment that Rufinus's translation of *De principiis* is reliable aside from Rufinus's own admission in his preface that he thought some passages on the Trinity were heretical and replaced them with texts from others of Origen's works. For support, Crouzel refers to Robinson's findings upon comparing the available Greek texts in the *Philocalia* with the corresponding Latin by Rufinus (also mentioned above), that, though paraphrastic, Rufinus had not changed much of the Greek text. See Robinson, *The Philocalia of Origen*, xxiv. Scholarship today tends to rely on Rufinus's translation even to understand Origen's views on the Holy Spirit and the Trinity. For example, in a recent, very fruitful study of the Holy Spirit (and the Spirit's relationship to the Father and Son) within Origen's *Comm in Rom*, Maureen Beyer Moser relies extensively upon Rufinus's translation after noting his own admitted alterations and the state of scholarship on Rufinus's reliability. See Maureen Beyer Moser, *Teacher of Holiness: The Holy Spirit in Origen's Commentary on the Epistle to the Romans*, Gorgias Dissertations 17, Early Christian Studies 4 (Piscataway, NJ: Gorgias Press, 2005), esp. 6–13.

24. Rufinus, *Preface to De Principiis* 1.3, cited by Heine, FOTC 71:35 n. 180. See also Rufinus, *Epilogue to Comm in Rom*, 4, in *Origen: Commentary on the Epistle to the Romans, Books 6–10*, trans. Thomas P. Scheck, FOTC 104, vol. 2 of 2 vols. (Washington, DC: The Catholic University of America Press, 2002), 312–13.

25. Rufinus, *Preface to De Principiis* 3, and *Preface to Heraclius*, cited by Heine, FOTC 71:35 n. 181. See also Rufinus, *Epilogue to Comm in Rom* 4, FOTC 104:312–13.

in the case of *Comm in Rom*, Rufinus claims that his benefactors wish the Greek text to be cut in half before making it available to the Latin audience.[26] Thus Rufinus, in addition to trying to capture the sense of the text rather than render a word-for-word translation, omits statements that he believes have been added by heretics, adds text that he believes corrects the heretical alterations or clarifies Origen's thought, and tries to make the Latin text shorter than the original Greek and thus more accessible to the Latin audience.

With specific regard to the homilies on Judges, Rufinus asserts, in his epilogue to *Comm in Rom*, that he found no need to alter them in any way:

[I]n the others that we have translated into Latin at your insistence, or rather, at your exaction of a daily work quota, there was no lack of very great effort, as we sought to supply things that were discussed by Origen extemporaneously in the lecture hall of the Church, his intention being not so much commentary as edification. This is what we did in the homilies, or brief sermons, on Genesis and on Exodus, and especially in those on the book of Leviticus that were dictated by him in a hortatory style, but translated by us into the form of a commentary. This was the reason we took the trouble of filling in things that were missing, lest the investigations he strikes up and abandons frustrate the Latin reader, since in the homiletical style of speaking this is frequently customary for him. For what we have written on Joshua son of Nun, and on Judges, and on the Thirty-sixth, Thirty-seventh, and Thirty-eighth Psalms, we translated just as we found them, literally and without great effort.[27]

Rufinus confirms what he has stated elsewhere, that he has "filled in" places within some homiletic texts where he deemed it necessary to make the work more intelligible to his Latin audience as well as to make them more like commentaries in their flow and less choppy and offensively hortatory as spoken sermons might be. But he stresses that he did not go to such efforts with Origen's homilies on Joshua, Judges, and the Psalms. Though he does not state why, Rufinus clarifies that he left these homilies virtually unaltered. This admission could suggest that Rufinus translated these three sets of homilies word-

26. Rufinus, *Preface to Comm in Rom* 2, FOTC 103:51–52.
27. Rufinus, *Epilogue to Comm in Rom* 1–2, FOTC 104:311.

for-word and did not paraphrase them. Whether Rufinus meant this or not,[28] we assume from this statement that for the homilies on Judges he did not find it necessary to delete from, add to, fill in, or shorten them, and, by implication, Rufinus believed that heretics had not tampered with them. So whether we have in the homilies on Judges Origen's exact expression or just the sense of his thought, both Rufinus's own words and the views of recent scholars suggest that we have an accurate translation of Origen's work without much, if any, doctoring by Rufinus.[29]

---

28. Heine does not believe that we should understand by Rufinus's statement in his epilogue to *Comm in Rom* that he translated the homilies on Joshua, Judges, and Psalms word-for-word. Heine defers to the work of translator and editor Annie Jaubert, in *Origène: Homélies sur Josué*, SC 71 (1960; reprinted and corrected, 2000), 75–82, whose extensive study of the homilies on Joshua, based especially on a comparison of *Hom in Jos* 20 with the Greek text in *Philocalia* 12, determined that Rufinus was quite faithful to the Greek, though in places he did insert thoughts from other works by Origen and in other places added an explanation of Origen's point in order to make it clearer and more effective for his Latin audience. See Heine, FOTC 71:37 n. 189. Bruce, translator of the Joshua homilies for FOTC, also defers to Jaubert's analysis and general conclusion that Rufinus was faithful to the thought and intention of Origen in those homilies, giving her own summary of Jaubert's findings. See Bruce, FOTC 105:17–18. For other scholars who find Rufinus's paraphrastic style reliable for Origen's own ideas and thought, see Wagner, *Rufinus, the Translator*, 11, 29, 35, 98, and J. E. L. Oulton, "Rufinus's Translation of the Church History of Eusebius," 157, both cited by Bruce, FOTC 105:17 n. 67. Also, as stated in text above, in an early, more general study, Robinson compared all the Greek in the *Philocalia* with Rufinus's corresponding Latin and found that Rufinus, though generally periphrastic in his approach, had not changed much. Robinson, *The Philocalia of Origen*, xxiv.

29. Heine thinks that even Rufinus's translations of the homilies on Genesis, Exodus, and Leviticus remain true to Origen's thought. Heine summarizes that (1) Rufinus is true to Origen's sense and meaning but not his exact words, (2) Rufinus may have changed the homiletic style to more of a commentary by filling in unexplained or unanswered points that Origen raised in his extemporaneous presentation, and (3) Rufinus may have cleaned up contradictions he thought to be heretical interpolations, especially concerning the Trinity and resurrection of the body, but on other theological points Rufinus's translation reliably provides Origen's own thought even in the homilies that he admittedly doctored. Heine, FOTC 71:37–38. As mentioned earlier, there is recent precedence for relying on Rufinus even for Origen's views of the Holy Spirit and the Trinity. See, for example, Moser, *Teacher of Holiness*.

INTRODUCTION 13

THE LIKELY DATES OF ORIGEN'S HOMILIES ON JUDGES

Both the major events of Origen's life and the history of scholarship on the dating of his whole homiletic opus generally tend to establish that his delivery of the homilies on Judges occurred sometime between 238 and 248. To reach this conclusion, we should first explore the tumultuous and peaceful periods for Christians in which Origen lived.

Born c. 185, Origen was raised by a Christian father, Leonides, who taught him both Scripture and Platonic philosophy.[30] He was only sixteen (c. 201) when his father was martyred in the first of three major persecutions against Christians that occurred during Origen's lifetime.[31] This first persecution was directed by Septimius Severus and lasted another ten years until Severus's death (c. 211). Though Origen strongly wished to be martyred for the faith with his father, his mother hid his clothes during his bath time, thus preventing this outcome. Instead, Origen began to teach the Christian faith to novices in his hometown of Alexandria to support his mother and siblings.

After Septimius Severus's death, Christians enjoyed relative peace in the Roman Empire for about twenty-four years until Maximin the Thracian (or Maximinus Thrax) became emperor and led a persecution against the Christians from c. 235 to 238. Not long before Maximin's persecution, c. 232, Origen, on a trip from Alexandria to Athens, stopped in Caesarea of Palestine, where the local bishop ordained him a presbyter so that he could preach before Church audiences, a privilege that the bishop of Alexandria had not afforded him. After completing

30. For a fuller outline of the major events marking Origen's life, see Eusebius, *Hist. eccl.* 6, trans. Arthur Cushman McGiffert, in Nicene and Post-Nicene Fathers, 2d series, 1, ed. Philip Schaff and Henry Wace (Peabody, MA: Hendrickson Publishers, 1994; reprinted from 1890), 249–92; and Nautin, *Origène*, 409–12. Note, however, that Nautin's dating of Origen's homilies between 238 and 244, based on the assumption that they were all delivered in the same three-year cycle, has been contested by more recent scholarship, as explained below.

31. For the three major persecutions, see generally Crouzel, *Origen*, 1–36. For Origen's likely age at the time of his father's death, see Eusebius, *Hist. eccl.* 6.1, n. 1, trans. McGiffert, NPNF2, 1, 249, and Nautin, *Origène*, 409, and note 41 below.

his travels, though, Origen found it necessary to go into hiding during Maximin's persecution, which, though "limited in its range," targeted Christianity in certain provinces as "a secret, and therefore a dangerous, society, the natural focus of conspiracies and plots."[32] Origen fled for safety to Caesarea in Cappadocia, where, in hiding, he wrote the *Exhortation to Martyrdom*. In this treatise he promotes physical martyrdom—if one is "blessed" enough to be faced with it—as well as a spiritual type of martyrdom that every Christian should pursue at all times by stripping himself of sinful ways and growing in the virtues. (This second theme of spiritual martyrdom is common throughout all of Origen's works, including the homilies on Judges, and so can be considered a focus of his during all periods—whether persecution-laden or peaceful.)

After Maximin, Origen returned to Caesarea of Palestine, and Christians generally enjoyed peace first under Gordian from 238 to 244 and then under Philip the Arabian, considered the first Christian emperor, from 244 to 249. This peace ended when Decius became emperor and ordered the first universal (that is, empire-wide) persecution against Christians between 249 and 251. Decius "ordered" leaders throughout the empire to "pressure" Christians, "under heavy penalties," including torture and death, to reject the faith.[33] This persecution "was more extensive and more systematic than any that had preceded it," and "there was hardly a province of the empire where the persecution was not felt."[34] Indeed, there were no safe regions in the empire to which to flee from this attack, and during this final major persecution of Origen's life scholars believe that Origen, as an old man, was captured and tortured and eventually died from his wounds in 254.[35]

If Origen was not ordained until 232, then he could not have

32. See "Maximinus (2) I" in *A Dictionary of Christian Biography*, ed. Henry Wace and William C. Percy (Peabody, MA: Hendrickson Publishers, 1994), 709–10.

33. See "Decius" in *A Dictionary of Christian Biography*, 248–50.

34. Ibid., 249.

35. Eusebius of Caesarea, in *Hist. eccl.* 6.39.5, reports that Origen was tortured for the faith during the Decian persecution and died afterwards, in ill health from the wounds inflicted. Recent scholars tend to rely on this report,

preached before Church audiences until after that date.[36] Moreover, according to Pierre Nautin, he did not begin preaching in Caesarea of Palestine until after his extensive travels between 232 and 235 and his period of refuge in Cappadocia during the persecution of Maximin between 235 and 238.[37] Nautin thus places the earliest year of Origen's preaching of any transcribed homilies at 238.[38] On the basis of his own idea of the three-year liturgical cycle at Origen's time, Nautin assumes that Origen preached all the transcribed homilies in the same three-year cycle, which he conjectures took place sometime between 238 and 244.[39]

Eusebius, the fourth-century Church historian, however, places all of Origen's homilies later in his life. He reports that Origen "never before allowed" his homilies to be transcribed until after he was sixty years old, when finally he believed that he had "gained great facility by his long practice."[40] If, as most scholars do, one assumes Origen was born around 185, he did not turn sixty until 245,[41] and thus he would not have delivered his transcribed homilies until after 245.

---

such as, for example, Greer, *Origen*, 4–5; Crouzel, *Origen*, 33–36; and Trigg, *Origen*, 61.

36. Over 200 of Origen's homilies are extant (279 total and 204 intact), mostly in Rufinus of Aquileia's or Jerome's Latin. There are 12 homilies on Jeremiah that are extant in the original Greek language as well as in Jerome's Latin translation. See Nautin, *Origène*, 401–5, and Heine, FOTC 71:21–24. Cf. Hanson, *Tradition*, 22.

37. Nautin does not place delivery before 238, since Origen's ordination to the presbyterate (and thus his license to preach before Church audiences) would not have occurred until 232, when he stopped in Caesarea of Palestine on the way from Alexandria to visit Greece, then went to Athens and returned to Caesarea of Palestine in 234, only to depart from 235 to 237 or 238 for Cappadocia, where he took refuge from the persecution under Maximin the Thracian. Nautin, *Origène*, 410–11. Origen, then, would not have begun to preach in Caesarea of Palestine until the persecutions under Maximin had ended and he was safely back in Caesarea of Palestine at the start of peace under Emperor Gordian in 238.

38. See Nautin, *Origène*, 411.

39. Ibid.

40. Eusebius, *Hist. eccl.* 6.36.1.

41. Scholars generally understand Origen's birth to have occurred in 185 or 186 A.D., given Eusebius's report that Origen was "not quite seventeen years

Scholars disagree on the reliability of Eusebius's statement. Accepting this statement, Crouzel places most of Origen's transcribed homilies after 245,[42] with the claim that all were generated during the peaceful period under Emperor Philip the Arabian between 244 and 249.[43] Crouzel points out that Philip "showed ... favor ... to the Christians," which caused many people to join the Church[44] in order to strengthen their favor with the state. Crouzel cites this as the cause of Origen's occasional expressions of frustration in some of the homilies at the growing moral and spiritual laxity of churchgoers.[45]

On the other hand, Nautin and Heine reject the accuracy of Eusebius's statement, and date many of Origen's works earlier than 245 or 246, on the basis of certain cross-references in Origen's works. As stated above, Nautin combines this argument with his assumption that Origen delivered all of the transcribed homilies within a single three-year cycle, before 245, during the earlier peaceful period under Emperor Gordian (238–244).[46]

---

old" (that is, 16, almost 17) at the time of his father's death under the persecution of Septimius Severus in "the tenth year of the reign of Severus, while Laetus was governor of Alexandria and the rest of Egypt, and Demetrius had lately received the episcopate of the parishes there, as successor of Julian," and given that the tenth year of Severus's reign was 201 or 202 A.D. See Eusebius, *Hist. eccl.* 6.1, n. 2, and 6.2, trans. McGiffert, NPNF2, 1, 249–50 and 391–92 (supplemental notes on "Origen's Life and Writings"), citing Redepenning I, 417–20, Erste Beilage.

42. See Crouzel, *Origen,* 29–30. Similarly, R. P. C. Hanson, in his earlier work from 1954, places the majority of the extant homilies between 246 and 255. See R. P. C. Hanson, *Origen's Doctrine of Tradition* (London: SPCK, 1954), 1–30, esp. 15 and 27. Hanson explores cross-references within Origen's works to determine more specific dates for particular sets of homilies, but he insists that they all occur in or later than 246. Hanson does suggest that some homilies do not read as transcribed by shorthand from deliveries to Church audiences but seem instead to have been written down earlier in Origen's career perhaps for use later before Church audiences: for example, the homilies on Luke, which Hanson dates as written in 233–234. See Hanson, *Tradition,* 21–22 and 26–27.

43. Crouzel, *Origen,* 3–4.

44. Crouzel, *Origen,* 4.

45. Ibid. Crouzel does not give any example with this statement, but one clear example of Origen admonishing his audience members for laxity is in *Hom in Gn* 11.3 (FOTC 71:174).

46. The dates Nautin offers for Origen's various works are based on cross-

INTRODUCTION 17

With regard to the dating of Origen's homilies on Judges specifically, Nautin relies on a phrase within Origen's prologue to his commentary on the Song of Songs: "the little addresses that we published on the Book of Judges."[47] He believes this phrase refers to the homilies on Judges as already published works.[48] R. P. C. Hanson expressly disagrees, arguing that it refers to "little addresses" on the song of Deborah within Judges that Origen may have written earlier in his career for the purpose of using later in his life as sermons.[49] Nonetheless, if we follow Nautin's train of thought, we see that he surmises that Origen completed the first four books, along with the prologue, of *Comm in Song* during his second trip to Athens in 245 and the last six books once he arrived back in Caesarea sometime between 246 and 247,[50] concluding that the homilies on Judges had to occur be-

---

references within Origen's works as well as information gathered from the following sources: Eusebius, *Hist. eccl.* 6, and Pamphilus, *Defense of Origen*. After surveying all of these early sources, however, Nautin bases his table of dates (Nautin, *Origène*, 409–12) on educated conjectures. Nautin's dates for the delivery of the transcribed homilies are also based on the assumption that all extant homilies were delivered during the same three-year liturgical cycle, an assumption from which some scholars have diverged. Also, Nautin believes that Origen's transcribed homilies on the Old Testament reflect that he began his preaching in the middle of a liturgical cycle starting with the Psalms, then working through the rest of the sapiential books, then working through the major prophets, and then working through the historical texts of the Pentateuch (beginning with Genesis), and finally Joshua, Judges, and 1 Samuel. Nautin, *Origène*, 403. Heine agrees with Nautin's general date of 238–244 for the delivery of Origen's extant homilies on the Old Testament. See Heine, FOTC 71:21–24.

47. *Comm in Song*, Prol. 4.9. See *Origen: The Song of Songs Commentary and Homilies*, ACW 26, trans. R. P. Lawson (New York and Ramsey, NJ: Newman Press, 1956), 49, and *Origène: Commentaire sur le Cantique des Cantiques*, ed. and trans. Luc Bresard, Henri Crouzel, and Marcel Borret, SC 375 (Paris: Cerf, 1991), 153.

48. See Nautin, *Origène*, 402.

49. See Hanson, *Tradition*, 22, and n. 40 above.

50. Nautin cites Eusebius, *Hist. eccl.* 6.32.2, for Athens as the place where Origen wrote *Comm in Song*. Nautin, *Origène*, 404 n. 111. McGiffert, translator of Eusebius's *Hist. eccl.*, interprets, in NPNF2, vol. 1, 277 n. 1, Eusebius's understanding of the timing of the trip to Athens as occurring during the reign of Gordian from 238 to 244. Translator of *Comm in Song*, R. P. Lawson, following a particular comment by Eusebius, places the first five books of the commen-

fore 245.⁵¹ On the basis of these dates, Nautin places the delivery of the homilies on Judges late in his assumed range for the homilies, at the start of 244.⁵² Of course, this analysis assumes that the prologue was written and published along with the first grouping of books on *Comm in Song*, yet no particular attention is paid to the dating of the prologue itself, and it is worth considering that Origen may have written the prologue after the completion of all ten books.

More recent scholarship departs from Nautin's assumption that the transcribed homilies were all delivered in the same three-year cycle, preferring to examine each set of homilies according to their own internal indicators of specific content as well as cross-references. On the basis of this reasoning, it is likely that Origen delivered the homilies on Judges *after* he delivered the homilies on Joshua, because in *Hom in Jgs* 3.3 Origen states that he has discussed with the Church audience previously the man Caleb, whom he discussed in detail in *Hom in Jos* 18 and 20.3–6. Now, Murphy and Barbara J. Bruce both favor dating the delivery of Origen's homilies on Joshua during Decius's empire-wide persecution between 249 and 250.⁵³ They rely on a sentence at the end of *Hom in Jos* 9, which they argue describes the Decian persecution as an event in progress,⁵⁴ as well as on

---

tary in 240 during an earlier trip that Origen took to Athens, and the latter five books sometime later when he was back in Caesarea. See Lawson, *Origen: The Song of Songs Commentary and Homilies*, ACW 26:4, referring to Eusebius of Caesarea, *Hist. eccl.* 6.32.2.

51. Nautin, *Origène*, 411. 52. Nautin, *Origène*, 404–5.

53. See Murphy, *Rufinus of Aquileia*, 190 n. 17, and Bruce, FOTC 105:19, and specifically n. 75.

54. "For the kings of the earth have assembled together, the senate and the people and the leaders of Rome, to blot out the name of Jesus and Israel at the same time. For they have decreed in their laws that there be no Christians. Every city, every class, attacks the name of Christians. But just as at that time all those kings assembling against Jesus were able to do nothing, so even now, whether princes or those opposing authorities, they have been able to do nothing to prevent the race of Christians from being propagated more widely and profusely." Origen, *Hom in Jos* 9.10 (trans. Bruce, FOTC 105:107). The language in this passage arguably refers to a universal, empire-wide ban on Christianity and persecution of its proponents such as occurred under Decius. (Nautin does not believe that this statement in *Hom in Jos* 9.10 refers to the Decian persecution, because there is no mention of martyrs and no call to remain firm for

INTRODUCTION 19

Rufinus's reference in the preface to Origen as *senex,* or "old," at the time.⁵⁵ Still, Bruce does not join Murphy without qualification, since she observes places within the homilies on Joshua where Origen reprimands his audience for being lax, a criticism that scholars might associate more with a time of peace than a time of persecution.⁵⁶

With regard to the homilies on Judges, Origen does speak enthusiastically of physical martyrdom in *Hom in Jgs* 7.⁵⁷ He encourages outward martyrdom or "baptism of blood," stressing that this second baptism makes its fortunate recipient immune from committing any further sin (unlike the recipient of the baptism of water).⁵⁸ Yet he does not, as he seems to do in *Hom in Jos* 9, refer in *Hom in Jgs* to an ongoing persecution. The praise of physical martyrdom in *Hom in Jgs* 7 may be viewed as fitting with the emphases of the other homilies on Judges, which stress the battle that ensues for the human soul and the believer's need to engage in that fight by imitating Christ through the virtues. We might understand that Origen simply adds to this battle theme in *Hom in Jgs* 7 by stressing that the believer who is given the blessed opportunity of physical martyrdom also imitates Christ by submitting to an experience directly akin to his Passion.

Given the significance of the empire-wide persecution to the state of the Church in the Decian period—not to mention Origen's personal fervor for martyrdom—one would expect direct references to actual martyrdoms in the context of the homilies. Since there is no indication in the homilies on Judges of an ongoing, contemporaneous persecution, it is reasonable to place

---

the faith if put under trial, both of which he assumes Origen would articulate if he were actually addressing an audience under a direct and current threat of persecution. Nautin, *Origène,* 401–2.) Bruce points out that in *Hom in Jos* 5.1 there is a suggestion of ongoing persecution as well: "Also we must hasten [to cross over the Jordan] so that we may pass through the burden of persecution with the virtue of patience." See Origen, *Hom in Jos* 5.1, referring to Jos 4.10–11 (FOTC 105:60), cross-referenced by Bruce, FOTC 105:107 n. 74.

55. See Rufinus, Preface to *Hom in Jos* in Bruce, trans., FOTC 105:24 and 24 n. 5.

56. See Bruce, trans., FOTC 105:20 n. 76, referring to *Hom in Jos* 10.1, as well as 1.7, 10.3, and 21.1.

57. See *Hom in Jgs* 7.2.   58. Ibid.

the outer limit of their delivery just before the Decian persecution, in 248, and thus the homilies on Joshua along with them. Therefore, the best hypothesis, without further study, for dating the homilies on Judges would suggest a time between 238 and 248, and, if we choose to rely on Eusebius's statement that Origen allowed their transcription only after he was a seasoned preacher, we can narrow the range to sometime between 245 and 248.

ORIGEN'S AUDIENCE FOR THE HOMILIES

As described above (and as considered more thoroughly in the theology section below), Origen provides his audience with the tools from Scripture that make it possible to shun sin and grow in virtue and so become imitators of Christ and, eventually, his eternal companions. Who comprises the audience for his homilies on Judges? While we cannot verify the answer to this question historically—further historical studies, as well as rhetorical and other literary analyses of the texts, are warranted to answer it—a preliminary review of the texts suggests that his audience could consist of believers at all levels of spiritual growth.

On the one hand, the homilies are relevant to Church leaders and teachers. The theme of the soul's struggle between virtue and vice certainly has significance for these shepherds of souls. In *Hom in Jgs* 8.5 Origen goes beyond discussing this theme generally to speak directly about the responsibilities of the preacher in this battle between virtue and vice, describing the preacher's duty to wash the feet of his hearers' souls with the grace of scriptural teaching in order to prepare them for the battle against vices and the Devil. Such themes and passages suggest that Origen considered his audience to encompass preachers.

In addition, these homilies involve, for the most part, allegorical interpretation of the senses of Scripture.[59] The interpretation of allegorical, or non-literal (psychic and pneumatic) levels of meaning were generally left to those who were more advanced in the faith, and in *De principiis* 4, Origen explains that a

---

59. See the following sections for a description of this method and Origen's application of it in these homilies.

person acquires access to the insights and benefits of Scripture's three senses in a progressive manner: that is, first, the literal sense; second, the psychic sense; and only third, the pneumatic sense.[60] Thus one could surmise that the use of such advanced exegesis further suggests that his audience consisted, at least in part, of teachers and preachers.

On the other hand, there is no need to presume that these homilies were exclusively addressed to such leaders. We know that in other circumstances where Origen prepared materials exclusively for Church leaders, his prose is indicative of this fact.[61] No such limitation is made in these homilies. And though Origen uses the higher, allegorical senses in these homilies, one cannot presume that this usage excludes the spiritually less advanced from his audience. At the very least, Origen might have hoped the less advanced would be able to grasp some portion of his presentation. Perhaps Origen understood that, since he grasped all three senses, as preacher he was responsible for teaching their insights to everyone else. If so, then, Origen arguably presented psychic and pneumatic readings whenever he could articulate them, offering them indiscriminately to a mixed audience of novice and advanced believers in the hope that each hearer would take what he could from the exegetical treatment. Moreover, even passages that address the role of the preacher have relevance to the lay audience, as these passages describe their relationship to these leaders.

Most significantly, the general theme of the struggle between

60. Origen also refers to this progressive advancement in understanding Scripture in *Hom in Gn* 2 and 11, *Hom in Lv* 5, and *Hom in Nm* 9. For commentary, see Dively Lauro, *The Soul and Spirit of Scripture*, 94–130. Also, here, in *Hom in Jgs* 5.6 and 6.2, Origen stresses progressive advancement in understanding Scripture's truths generally.

61. For example, Origen clearly addresses Church leaders—preachers and teachers—in *De principiis* 4, where he sets forth his threefold method of scriptural interpretation. See Dively Lauro, *The Soul and Spirit of Scripture*, 38–47, as well as Karen Jo Torjesen, *Hermeneutical Procedure and Theological Method in Origen's Exegesis*, Patristische Texte und Studien 28 (Berlin and New York: Walter de Gruyter, 1986), 39–40, and Brian E. Daley, "Origen's *De Principiis:* A Guide to the Principles of Christian Scriptural Interpretation," *Nova et Vetera: Patristic Studies in Honor of Thomas Patrick Halton*, ed. John Petruccione (Washington, DC: The Catholic University of America Press, 1998), 3–21 (especially 15–16).

virtue and vice is certainly relevant to any individual Christian, no matter how spiritually learned. If we can assume that Origen presented these homilies in a Church setting, we should expect that his audience contained people in varying degrees of spiritual advancement.

In fact, we could even see how the uninitiated (catechumens) could fall within Origen's audience. Although nowhere in these homilies is there a direct address to catechumens,[62] a review of the liturgical cycle during Origen's time suggests that at least sometimes, and perhaps always, catechumens were included in his audience. Based on a variety of ancient sources, Nautin provides a likely picture of the weekly liturgy in the Church during Origen's time.[63] He surmises that on all days of the week except Sunday there was a morning worship service without Eucharist that included a lengthy reading and homily on an Old Testament text. This service would be open to catechumens as well as those more advanced in the faith.[64] Catechumens, however, would not have been present during the celebration of the Eucharist, and they also were generally excluded from the reading of the Gospel unless they were in the last weeks before their baptism.[65] On Wednesdays and Fridays Christians fasted, with

62. In contrast, Origen directly addresses catechumens in other homilies on Old Testament texts *(Hom in Jos* 4.1 and 9.9) as well as on Gospel texts *(Hom in Lk* 21.4, 22.8, and 32.5).

63. Nautin, *Origène,* 391–401. Nautin cites his ancient sources for the weekly liturgical schedule as follows: Socrates, *Church History* 5; *Didache;* Justin Martyr, *Apology* (esp. 1.67); the *Apostolic Tradition;* the works of Tertullian; and Origen's own works. See also Heine, trans., FOTC 71:19–21, for a general agreement with and summary of Nautin's explanation of the liturgical cycle.

64. Heine, trans., FOTC 71:20 n. 114, cites *Hom in Jos* 4.1, in which Origen seems to address beginners in the faith who are recent catechumens or about to be accepted into the Church as catechumens, informing them of the process ahead in which they will hear the divine law and then be ready for baptism and finally all of the sacraments administered by the priests. After progressing this far, the faithful will be received by Jesus, who will lead them the rest of the way on their journey toward spiritual perfection. See Origen's text in FOTC 105:52–53.

65. See Heine, Introduction, FOTC 71:20, citing *Apostolic Tradition* 20. As stated above in note 62, there are direct addresses to catechumens in some of the homilies on Luke. These, then, would have been seasoned catechumens approaching their baptisms within a matter of weeks or less.

the fast ending at an evening service that included readings and homilies on Old Testament and Gospel texts followed by Eucharist. On Sunday mornings there was a service with short readings and homilies on texts from the Old Testament, the apostolic letters or the book of Acts, and the Gospels, all followed by Eucharist. With this regimen, services could cover the entire Old Testament over a three-year period, which was also the time frame for a catechumen's preparation for baptism and full initiation into the Church.[66]

Whether catechumens were invited to all readings of the Old Testament and then simply dismissed before the Gospel readings (unless close to baptism) and Eucharist is not known. If, however, study of the Hebrew Scriptures' significance to the Christian faith was integral to preparation for baptism and initiation, then novices were likely included at all readings of the Old Testament and dismissed only afterwards if Gospel and Eucharist followed. Further, if we assume that Origen preached whenever needed, including the morning services that excluded Eucharist and occurred daily except Sundays, then we must consider that at least some of the time catechumens were present to hear him.

Of course, such an analysis may be overly simplistic. It is possible that Origen addressed different subgroups within his audience with different points in his homilies. Furthermore, we cannot be sure that the texts we are reviewing provide us direct insight into the original audience of Origen's homilies for two reasons: first, we do not know that Origen had them transcribed word-for-word as they might have originally been presented in churches, and, second, we do not have Origen's original text, but rather that of Rufinus, who purportedly prepared these translations with a later, Latin audience in mind. With respect to the first caveat, it is completely possible that Origen, when transcribing, or overseeing the transcription of, the homilies, revised them in a manner that addressed the needs of an audience other than his original hearers, namely, other educated Church leaders. With respect to the second caveat, Rufinus, although reliable in translating Origen from a "big picture"

---

66. Nautin, *Origène,* 401. See also Heine, FOTC 71:20, citing *Apostolic Tradition* 17.

perspective, proclaimed (as discussed above) that he tended to simplify the complexity of the original Greek transcription in an effort to make Origen more relevant to his Latin readers.

These are open questions for future scholars to consider. Nonetheless, it is possible to approach the text that we have received and to analyze the audience of *that* text, regardless of whether or not it is consistent with the audience to which Origen originally preached. And, as we describe above, it is possible for the audience of the extant text to constitute a broad range of believers. Further study in terms of historical and rhetorical analysis is merited in order to consider just how varied Origen's audience was for these particular homilies on Judges.

ORIGEN'S EXEGETICAL METHOD

Origen, known in the history of the Christian Church as the father of scriptural interpretation, solidly established the relevance of the Hebrew Scriptures to the Christian faith by applying the allegorical method of interpretation to a prodigious number of texts. We should expect him to use this method in his homilies on Judges, and an overview of this method is merited. Briefly, his allegorical approach involves seeing the major elements of Christian faith in non-literal or figurative readings of text. In addition, Origen often relies upon typology in these allegories by finding an historical person in the Hebrew Scriptures to foreshadow (to be a "type" of) Christ or a person in the New Testament, or an historical event to be a type of some event related to Christ or the Church established upon his death.[67] By using this typology, Origen is able to draw a

---

67. Modern scholars debate the difference between allegory and typology, stressing that the former dismisses the importance of the historical or literal meaning of the text, while the latter explicitly relies upon it. For Origen, however, this modern debate is of minimal significance, since he draws on allegorical and typological readings freely and often in relation to one another. He draws allegorical meaning from texts that he perceives to be historically or literally true as well as texts that he believes hold no literal significance, and he understands many figures and events of the Hebrew Scriptures to be types of Christ and the future events of his life, death, and resurrection, and the establishment of the Church and its practices. See "Allegory"

Christian understanding of salvation history out of Scripture, with the persons and events of the Hebrew Scriptures serving as types of persons and events in the New Testament or persons and events relating to the victory of Christ and his bride, the Church, at the Eschaton, or end of time.

Early in his writing career, before his post as a preacher, Origen wrote *De principiis*. There he set forth not only the major tenets of Christian belief but also, in the fourth and last book of the treatise, his famous method of exegesis. He explains that every word of scriptural text is inspired by God and meant to direct the hearer or reader to spiritual perfection and thus prepare him for salvation, or eternal union with God. Christ, the ultimate content and teacher of Scripture, guides the attentive hearer to God's own truths through three senses of meaning (one literal and two allegorical) within scriptural texts.[68] The literal (somatic or bodily) sense offers historical information concerning God's faithfulness to mankind (such as when he leads the Jews through the Red Sea and away from the enslaving grip of the Egyptians) or moral edification (such as the guiding principles of the Decalogue). Not every text is literally true and thus edifying. According to Origen, however, every text includes edi-

---

(John J. O'Keefe), *The Westminster Handbook to Origen*, ed. John Anthony McGuckin, 49–50. For a recent, careful consideration of the merits and the weaknesses of the contemporary discussion of the distinction between allegory and typology in studies of Origen's exegesis, see Peter W. Martens, "Revisiting the Allegory / Typology Distinction: The Case of Origen," *Journal of Early Christian Studies* 16.3 (Fall 2008): 283–317. Martens demonstrates that, while Origen does find improper non-literal interpretations of scriptural text, it is not (as contemporary scholars tend to argue) allegory per se that is improper and typology that is proper for Origen. Rather, Origen defies this simplistic demarcation of the terms, and finds legitimate allegorical as well as typological interpretations of scriptural texts and, at times, improper ones. Martens calls for readers of Origen to free him from this strict distinction between allegory and typology as improper versus proper, respectively. Indeed, I might add, Origen's spiritual aim causes him to approach Scripture as a rich mine that brings its saving truth to attentive hearers through the variety of means available.

68. For an extensive study of Origen's three senses of scriptural meaning, see Dively Lauro, *The Soul and Spirit of Scripture*. Also, for Origen's understanding of Christ as the teacher and the content of Scripture, see Torjesen, *Hermeneutical Procedure*, 108–47.

fication at two separate non-literal levels of meaning: the psychic (or soul's) meaning and the pneumatic (or spiritual) meaning. In *De principiis* 4 as well as in certain homilies,[69] Origen explains that the psychic sense calls the hearer to be aware of the constant battle that vices and virtues (as well as demons and angels) wage for possession of his soul.[70] This sense urges him to strive against the dark forces by shunning sin and growing in virtue in order to become like Christ and ready for salvation. The pneumatic sense is a second, separate non-literal meaning of the text. It informs the hearer of God's plan of salvation through Christ. More specifically, it focuses on Christ's Incarnation, death and resurrection, the Church's emerging role, and Christ's culminating power at the end of time.[71]

Each sense prepares the growing believer to grasp the next higher level of meaning: first the somatic, then the psychic, and ultimately the pneumatic. The advanced believer, however, receives continual edification from the interrelation of all three senses. Sometimes Origen offers both figurative meanings for the same biblical text in his homilies or other works, while at

69. For Origen's theoretical explanations of the three senses of scriptural meaning, see, in addition to *De principiis* 4, *Hom in Gn* 2 and 11, *Hom in Lv* 5, and *Hom in Nm* 9, as well as the commentary on each in Dively Lauro, *The Soul and Spirit of Scripture*, 94–130.

70. Within the homilies on Judges, Origen emphasizes both levels of spiritual combat for possession of the human soul. For him angels and demons are very real entities who fight on the spiritual plane for influence over the soul, the angels guarding and guiding souls, and the demons making every possible attack upon them. (See *Hom in Jgs* 3.3, 3.4–3.6, 6.2, and 7.1–7.2.) Yet, also for Origen, the tug-of-war between virtues and vices is a constant strain upon the human soul throughout this life. This battle between virtues and vices for the human soul is evident throughout Origen's homilies on Judges. See also "Angels" (Johan Leemans), "Demonology" (Fiona Thompson), and "Virtue" (Lillian Larsen), *The Westminster Handbook to Origen*, 51–53, 85–86, and 214–16. See also Greer, *Origen*, esp. 20–23.

71. One could view the four biblical senses of medieval exegesis as having their roots in Origen's three senses, with the literal or historical sense translating directly into the medieval literal sense, the psychic sense rendering the medieval tropological sense, and the pneumatic sense separating later into the medieval allegorical sense (concerning Christ's life and death and the Church on earth) and the medieval anagogical sense (concerning the victory of Christ and the Church at the end of time).

other times he offers only one. His choice is likely determined by the needs of his present audience (as well as, perhaps, his own ability at the time to grasp the deeper truths of certain scriptural texts).[72] Regardless, within Origen's exegesis both figurative senses complement each other. Together they stress that the struggle for spiritual growth is an ascent to Christ that can occur only within the Church.

THE MAJOR THEOLOGICAL THEMES IN THE NINE HOMILIES ON JUDGES

Let us examine how Origen treats specific texts to draw out the theological themes that he sees in these psychic and pneumatic messages for his audience in the homilies on Judges. We shall see that he develops several separate but related aspects of the theological theme based on the psychic sense and also develops the theological theme based on the pneumatic sense. Also, we shall see that the relationship between the two senses is an apparent means by which he brings spiritual edification to his hearers.

In the homilies on Judges, Origen's recurring theological theme based on the psychic sense is the ongoing battle between virtue and vice for possession of the human soul. Origen, as a spiritual director to the Church audience, fervently and repeatedly directs his audience to bear this in mind at all times. We draw on two examples here in order to see how he presents this theme to his audience. In *Hom in Jgs* 1 Origen interprets Jgs 2.7, which states that "the people served the Lord all the days of Jesus [son of Nun, namely, Joshua]" and "of the elders." He explains that a person lives either in the days of Jesus Christ and the apostles (of which Jesus son of Nun and the elders respectively are types), or in the wicked days of the Devil.[73] Then, applying a more internal focus, Origen states that there are either just days or evil days in a person, depending on whether he follows "the true light," Jesus, which "will never be extinguished,"

---

72. See *Hom in Nm* 27 for an admission by Origen that the deepest nonliteral truths of some texts still lie beyond his grasp.
73. *Hom in Jgs* 1.1.

or the fleeting light of the deceptive one who disguises himself as an angel of light but truly represents darkness.[74] The only way to ensure company with the "eternal light" is to pray that Jesus "make good days in us,"[75] that is, help us to grow in the virtues, each of which is a day of Jesus.[76]

A second example of Origen directing his audience to focus on the battle for the soul is when he treats the death of Jesus son of Nun (Jgs 2.8).[77] He warns his audience that the death of a good religious leader signals that Israel has become "unworthy" to enjoy peace before God.[78] They have abandoned God and returned to sin.[79] Indeed, in some people "Jesus lives," while in others he is "dead."[80] Jesus Christ is dead in those who sin, for sinning is equivalent to "crucifying" and "mocking" Jesus all over again within oneself.[81] If the virtues are dead in a person, then Jesus is dead in him as well.[82] As the Israelites after Jesus son of Nun's death "bowed down" to Baal and "abandoned" God, so a non-believer in Christ or a fallen believer bows down before idols, for a person serves either Christ through the virtues or the Devil through sins.[83] Origen urges his hearer to examine before whom he or she bows the "knees of his or her heart," and he assures the hearer that God will "hand you over" to your enemies, that is, to sins and the Devil, if that is what your heart chooses to worship.[84]

As mentioned before, the homilies contain numerous refer-

---

74. Ibid.
75. Ibid.
76. *Hom in Jgs* 1.3.
77. See *Hom in Jgs* 2.
78. *Hom in Jgs* 2.5. See also *Hom in Jgs* 3.3 for the idea that Israel became "worthy" of a savior sent by God once they cried out to God repentantly for help, as well as *Hom in Jgs* 3.4 for the idea that Israel became "unworthy" of their current savior (i.e., leader) when they began to sin again.
79. *Hom in Jgs* 2.3.
80. *Hom in Jgs* 2.1.
81. Ibid.
82. Ibid.
83. *Hom in Jgs* 2.2–5.
84. Ibid. While in the first homilies Origen encourages his audience to imitate Christ by growing in the virtues, in *Hom in Jgs* 7 he explains that the baptism of blood, or physical martyrdom, is a sure way to wash away all sins, past and future, and thus to complete the ascent to God. Still, this discussion fits with the general lesson of his psychic readings that the believer should strive to become worthy of God's grace and seek the path toward salvation that God affords him. See *Hom in Jgs* 7.2.

ences to the battle between vice and virtue for the human soul. Using the psychic sense, Origen develops at least three supporting components of this theological theme: one emphasizing God's limitless mercy and forgiveness, another pointing to God, and not the believer, as the one who ultimately facilitates victory for the soul, and a third in which Origen stresses that Scripture is the necessary guide for the spiritual battle.

When Origen develops the notion of God's mercy, he explains that it will come to the aid of anyone who turns to God—regardless of how many times he has abandoned God by relapsing into sin (Jgs 2–3).[85] In one place, he explains that because Israel "forgot the Lord," that is, ignored God,[86] they were handed over to King Cushanrishathaim of Mesopotamia, whose name means "humiliation."[87] God allows the sinful soul to embrace its idol, because the inevitable humiliation will serve as medicine against the pride that initially led the soul astray.[88] Origen entreats his audience to preempt this kind of suffering by humbling themselves and crying out to God repentantly, for then God will find them "worthy" to receive a savior[89] such as Othniel, whom God sent to release a repentant Israel from Cushanrishathaim.[90] Othniel is a figure or type of the "savior angels"[91] whom God sends to us when we need divine powers to fight off evil forces.[92] Of

---

85. See *Hom in Jgs* 3.

86. *Hom in Jgs* 3.1. The Latin term is *ignorabat* from *ignorare*, which can mean "to take no notice of," "to pay no attention to," "to ignore," or "to disregard." At times this translation renders the term into English as "did not know God" or "forgot God," with the understanding that Origen means that Israel, and, psychically, the sinner, *deliberately* turn their backs on God.

87. *Hom in Jgs* 3.3.

88. *Hom in Jgs* 3.1–2. Also, at the end of the second homily Origen stresses that God allows our unwise choices only in order to lead us ultimately to reform and salvation (*Hom in Jgs* 2.5). Origen also points out in that same passage that such measures apply not only to lapsing lay people but also to wayward Church leaders (*Hom in Jgs* 2.5).

89. *Hom in Jgs* 3.3. See also *Hom in Jgs* 2.5 and 3.6 for the idea of God withholding a savior from those who are "unworthy" (i.e., who sin) and sending a savior to those who are "worthy" (i.e., who have stopped sinning and instead cry out to God for help).

90. *Hom in Jgs* 3.2–3.

91. *Hom in Jgs* 3.3.

92. Ibid.

course, though, if after the aid, the soul, as Israel, sins again, it becomes "unworthy" and that savior will depart, just as for Israel, "Othniel died" when Israel began sinning again.[93] God's mercy is "abundant,"[94] however, Origen assures, and once the soul cries out to God again for help, God will send another savior, just as he sent Ehud to save Israel from bondage to King Eglon of Moab after they cried out for help.[95] Just as Ehud, with a sword, killed Eglon and freed Israel, God mercifully will defeat sin in our lives once we look to God for the solution.[96]

In places, Origen explains more specifically how God uses Church leaders to bring his mercy to repentant believers. He notes that after Ehud, Israel received Shamgar to free them from their latest captors, the Philistines (Jgs 4), but stresses that Shamgar overcame the Philistines with a plough.[97] While Ehud's sword represents the harsh words and admonitions that a Church leader must sometimes use to correct a sinful soul, the plough represents a subtler means of correction, a more "gentle admonition."[98] The Church leader, and indeed the believer himself, should be a farmer to his soul, ploughing it and thereby breaking it slowly over time so that the enemy vices in it will eventually die and the soul can begin to receive and nurture the seeds of virtue.[99]

Related to the notion of mercy is God's power to bring the soul to victory over vices and the Devil. While the discussions of God's mercy above also point to God's power to bring saviors in the form of angels or Church leaders to the aid of repentant souls, Origen in *Hom in Jgs* 9 focuses squarely on God's power as the one and only source of victory for the soul in the battle against the vices. He stresses for his audience the humility necessary in understanding and accepting that God, not the individual, always deserves the credit for winning a soul away from vices and the Devil. Origen treats Jgs 7, in which God reduces Gideon's army against the Midianites from 32,000 to 300 men[100] and orders as weapons jugs of water, lamps, and horned

---

93. *Hom in Jgs* 3.4. See also *Hom in Jgs* 2.5.
94. *Hom in Jgs* 3.2 and 3.3.
95. *Hom in Jgs* 3.5.
96. *Hom in Jgs* 3.6.
97. *Hom in Jgs* 4.2.
98. Ibid.
99. Ibid.
100. *Hom in Jgs* 9.1.

INTRODUCTION 31

war-trumpets.[101] God leads Gideon and his 300 men, armed with these items, to victory over the much more numerous Midianites, showing that God alone is to receive glory for the victory. Likewise, in the battle for the soul, if the believer prays and grows in the knowledge of Christ and the mystery of his cross that are found in Scripture,[102] God's grace will provide victory over the vices and the Devil.[103]

Ultimately, Origen's psychic readings always point to a third supporting message: God's saving power is always found in the Scriptures, so interaction with Scripture is essential to winning the battle for the soul against the vices and the Devil. At the end of the eighth homily, Origen stresses the role of the preacher in conveying to all believers Scripture's power to lead the hearer to imitation of Christ through cultivation of the virtues.[104] He likens Gideon's act of wringing the water out of the fleece into a basin (Jgs 6) to Jesus' wringing out a cloth into a basin and using it to wash his disciples' feet at the Last Supper. In turn, Origen stresses that he, as preacher, is called to wring out the dew of heavenly grace that is found in Scripture and to wash the feet of his hearers' souls with it.[105] As the judges and prophets in Judges are "types" of Jesus Christ, so the preacher and teacher of Scripture represents Christ, who, by delivering Scripture's truths, performs a baptism. The preacher washes the "feet" of his co-disciples'[106] souls as Jesus washed the feet of his disciples at the

---

101. *Hom in Jgs* 9.2.
102. Ibid. (specifically, in the last paragraph of the homily).
103. Ibid. (specifically, in the last paragraph of the homily).
104. Also, in the first homily, Origen stresses that Scripture directs the cultivation of the virtues, when he points out that even the apostolic examples and precepts in the New Testament writings prepare the hearer "to serve the Lord"; *Hom in Jgs* 1.2.
105. *Hom in Jgs* 8.5.
106. With the Latin term *condiscipulorum meorum* in *Hom in Jgs* 8.5, Origen refers to members of his audience and to fellow churchgoers literally as "my fellow disciples." It can also be translated as "my companions." In the same breath he also refers to them as *fratrum meorum*, or "my brothers." By this address, he places his audience and other Church members on an equal footing with himself. He suggests that we all, as fellow disciples of Christ, are responsible for washing the feet of each other's souls by the instruction and encouragement of Scripture's truths.

Last Supper. Understanding that Christ is both the content and ultimate teacher of Scripture,[107] Origen views the preacher as instrumental in preparing and ultimately presenting the soul to Christ for direct instruction. An encounter with Scripture purifies the soul of sin and directs it to take on virtues. Origen also urges each hearer to wash the feet of his own soul by hearing Scripture.[108] Still, always and ultimately it is Jesus himself reaching from the cross through Scripture to mend the sin-ridden soul and make it reflect himself through the virtues. As in baptism, this water of Scripture washes away sin and prepares the hearer's soul for the Gospel.[109] Ultimately, the soul who engages with Scripture will complete the salvific ascent and enter into the marriage chamber of the Bridegroom, Jesus Christ, where it will abide in his reflection for eternity.[110]

Origen in several places employs a pneumatic reading of texts within Judges that complements the theology developed by his psychic readings. This pneumatic reading stresses that the ascent toward spiritual maturity and salvation can take place only within the Church.[111] Two examples in the homilies on Judges help to demonstrate this pneumatic message.

At the end of the fourth[112] and throughout the fifth homily, Origen analyzes the fall of Sisera, the leader of Jabin's Philistine army, at the hands of a woman, Jael (Jgs 4). Sisera, whose name means "vision of the horse," represents the animal or unspiritual man who does not use intellect but runs after passions like a beast.[113] The Israelite pursuing Sisera is Barak. Barak, whose

107. See Dively Lauro, *The Soul and Spirit of Scripture,* and Torjesen, *Hermeneutical Procedure,* esp. 108–47.

108. *Hom in Jgs* 8.5.

109. The translator of this volume is presently at work on an article that treats *Hom in Jgs* 8 along with other works by Origen in order to establish and analyze the significance of his view that the preaching and reception of Scripture are sacramental acts that directly confer God's saving grace.

110. *Hom in Jgs* 8.5.

111. Origen also speaks in detail of the believer's ascent to the risen Christ through the Church in *Hom in Gn* 2 in which he provides an exegetical treatment of the dimensions and description of Noah's ark. See FOTC 71:72–88, trans. Heine. For commentary, see Dively Lauro, *The Soul and Spirit of Scripture,* 132–47.

112. *Hom in Jgs* 4.4. 113. *Hom in Jgs* 4.4 and 5.5.

name means "a flash,"[114] represents the impermanent light of the first chosen people of God. Because they do not believe in Jesus Christ, even though he is foretold at the spiritual level of meaning in their own Scriptures, they cannot ascend to salvation first.[115] Deborah, the prophetess-judge, whose name can mean "bee,"[116] represents the sweet honey of truth in Scripture that foretells God's saving plan for his people.[117] She tells Barak that God commands him to "go up Mount Tabor and take 10,000 men."[118] The men, though, will not go up unless Deborah goes with them, so she agrees but warns them that their "primacy" will not go up with them.[119]

Meanwhile, it is Jael, not Barak, who finds Sisera and lures him to the place where she can kill him for the salvation of Israel. Jael, whose name means "ascent,"[120] represents the Church.[121] Because of its belief in Christ, the Church is able to slay the enemy, the Devil, of whom Sisera is a type.[122] Jael's weapon, a stake, represents (is a type of) "the power of the wood of the Cross," with which she pierces Sisera's jaw, which signifies (is a type of) the falsehoods of the Epicurean praise of pleasure.[123] In conclusion, Origen points out, it is only through the Church that ascent to salvation occurs.[124] Yet he assures that the Jews will share in this salvation, but only because the Church first believed.[125]

In the eighth homily Origen gives another pneumatic reading of text that again emphasizes the role of the Church in God's plan of salvation. At Jgs 6.36–40, Gideon twice asks God to give him a sign—involving a fleece of wool on a threshing floor and the moisture of dew—that God will save Israel by

---

114. *Hom in Jgs* 5.4.
115. *Hom in Jgs* 5.3–4.
116. *Hom in Jgs* 5.2.
117. Ibid.
118. *Hom in Jgs* 5.4.
119. Ibid.
120. *Hom in Jgs* 5.5.
121. *Hom in Jgs* 5.4.
122. *Hom in Jgs* 5.5.
123. Ibid.
124. Ibid.
125. Ibid. But it is with a plea for hearing Scripture that Origen ends the fifth homily, when he points out that Jael gave Sisera milk before she put him to sleep forever. This milk represents the first principles of truth in the Gospels and apostolic letters that will put to sleep the Devil who resides within the sinner. See *Hom in Jgs* 5.6.

Gideon's hand[126] from its present enemies.[127] According to Origen, the fleece of wool represents the people of Israel, the rest of the ground the other nations, or gentiles, the dew the word of God,[128] and the threshing floor the place of the salvific harvest where Jesus will separate the grain from the chaff.[129] In the first sign, God, per Gideon's request, causes the fleece on the threshing floor to be wet with dew, but the rest of the ground to be dry. Origen explains that this first sign represents the Jews who were obedient to the Law before the coming of Christ.[130] They alone honored God's word. In the second sign, God also follows Gideon's request, this time leaving the fleece dry, but the rest of the ground wet with dew. This sign describes the Church's responsiveness to God's word, but the Jews' obstinacy after the coming of Christ.[131] As with Jael and Barak in Jgs 4, here Origen points out that God's ultimate act of salvation is through Christ and comes about because of the Church's belief despite the Jews' unbelief.[132] Therefore, the relationship between the psychic and pneumatic messages becomes clear: the soul's efforts to win the battle against vices and demons, with the God-given help of angels and Church leaders and especially the guidance of Christ himself through Scripture, can take place only within the Church.[133]

126. *Hom in Jgs* 8.4.
127. *Hom in Jgs* 8.1. The present trio of enemies that Gideon and the Israelites face are the Midianites, the Amalekites, and the people of the East, who, according to Origen, respectively are types of the pagans, of the non-believing Jews, and of the heretics of the Church's time, that is, of all those who attack the Church in one way or another.
128. *Hom in Jgs* 8.4. Origen claims that "predecessors" have already read the story of Gideon and the fleece at the spiritual (or pneumatic) level of meaning with the same typological representations that Origen employs. The predecessors to whom Origen refers are unknown. The same pneumatic reading, however, of Gideon's requests regarding the fleece—that juxtaposes Israel and the Church—is found after Origen in the work of Theodoret (c. 393–c. 466), Bishop of Cyrrhus, in his *Quaestiones in Iudices* 6, 15 (PG 80:501). See *Origène: Homélies sur Les Juges*, ed. and trans. Pierre Messié, Louis Neyrand, and Marcel Borret, SC 389 (Paris: Les Éditions du Cerf, 1993), 194 n. 1.
129. *Hom in Jgs* 8.5, referring to Mt 3.12.
130. *Hom in Jgs* 8.4. 131. Ibid.
132. Ibid.
133. Again, as stated in the text above, Origen is quick to point out that

INTRODUCTION 35

MANUSCRIPT HISTORY, EDITIONS, GUIDELINES
FOR THIS TRANSLATION

The definitive Latin edition for Origen's homilies on Judges was prepared by W. A. Baehrens in 1926.[134] For the manuscript tradition from the time of Rufinus's translation until Baehrens's edition, see Baehrens in TU 42[135] and Pierre Messié, Louis Neyrand, and Marcel Borret in SC 389.[136] Messié, Neyrand, and Borret present the same edition by Baehrens, *sans la modifier*, in the more recent publication of the Sources Chrétiennes series.[137] The present translation employs the Latin of the SC edition.[138]

The present translation follows the Latin as literally as possible, noting that many Latin words require interpretation within the context of their usage in order to determine the most adequate corresponding words in English. This translation follows the section and paragraph breaks of the SC edition, but occasionally diverges from the edition's sentence breaks where readability in English dictates. Any biblical text is translated literally from the Latin. All biblical names correspond to the RSV. All Old Testament citations correspond to the standard divisions of the LXX, which Origen is believed to have employed, but the RSV chapter and verse are noted where they differ from the LXX. All New Testament citations correspond to the RSV numeration.

---

the Jews will be saved as well in the end, but only because someone in history, indeed, the Church, has recognized God's final savior, Jesus Christ. See *Hom in Jgs* 5.5.

134. W. A. Baehrens, *Origenes Werke* VII, GCS 30.

135. W. A. Baehrens, *Ueberlieferung und Textegeschichte der lateinischen erhaltenen Origeneshomilien zum Alten Testament*, TU 42, 1 (1916), 186–99.

136. *Origène: Homélies sur Les Juges*, SC 389, 40–41.

137. Ibid., 41.

138. While the present translation is the first in English for Origen's homilies on Judges, the following are two other formidable, recent translations into modern languages: *Origène: Homélies sur Les Juges*, ed. and trans. Messié, Neyrand, and Borret, SC 389 (French), and *Origene: Omelie sui Giudici*, trans. Maria Ignazia Danieli (Rome: Città Nuova Editrice, 1992) (Italian).

HOMILIES ON JUDGES

HOMILY ONE

Concerning what is written in the Book of Judges:
"And the people served the Lord all the days of Jesus,
and all the days of the elders, as many as lived a
multitude of days after Jesus, who experienced
all the great works of the Lord
that he did for Israel."[1]

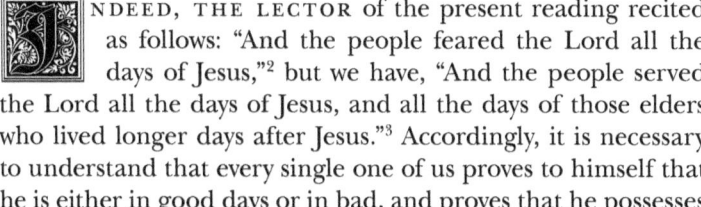NDEED, THE LECTOR of the present reading recited as follows: "And the people feared the Lord all the days of Jesus,"[2] but we have, "And the people served the Lord all the days of Jesus, and all the days of those elders who lived longer days after Jesus."[3] Accordingly, it is necessary to understand that every single one of us proves to himself that he is either in good days or in bad, and proves that he possesses either "the days of Jesus," that is, the days of the just, or the days of the wicked. For if we comprehend "the true light that enlight-

---

1. This homily treats Jgs 2.7. All scriptural texts are translated directly from the Latin translation of Origen's text. All references to the Hebrew Scriptures reflect chapter and verse in the Septuagint (LXX), and, where different, the RSV chapter and verse are set forth in parentheses. Likewise, biblical names of persons and places are consistent with the RSV.

2. As stated in the introduction, this translation of the homilies employs "Jesus" in English for Joshua son of Nun as well as for Jesus Christ, since "Jesus" accurately reflects the Latin (and the underlying Greek) and captures Origen's portrayal of Joshua as a type of Jesus Christ. Bruce, translator of Origen's homilies on Joshua, chose the same practice. See Bruce, FOTC 105:24 n. 4.

3. Jgs 2.7. Origen suggests here that he is using a text that differs from the liturgical text. Origen's following remarks suggest that he found the verb "to serve" to be more effective than "to fear" for the purpose of reading allegorically "the days of Jesus" as the virtues and "the days of the elders" as the apostles' precepts and examples recorded in Scripture.

ens[4] every man coming into this world"[5] and we offer our souls to it[6] in order to be enlightened, or if "the sun of justice"[7] rises up within us and "illuminates the world" of our soul, then we also possess the "days of Jesus" Christ, the days of salvation. But if someone offers his soul in order to receive that light which "will be extinguished,"[8] the light contrary to truth, and is illuminated by it, he also will himself possess days, but evil ones. He will not be in the days of Jesus, but he will be in the days of Manasseh or in the days of the Pharaoh or in wicked days of some other kind.[9] Accordingly, therefore, in the days of the unjust and wicked King Ahaz [Uzziah],[10] Isaiah could not see a vision. He could not "see the Lord of Hosts sitting upon the throne, high and lifted up."[11] But from the moment that vile king died, whose "days" were "evil,"[12] then the prophet was able to see a vision of God.

Also, do you wish to know why those days, when in Scripture they are said to be of that kind or the other kind, would not refer to the lifetime of that very one discussed, that is, the time

4. The verb *illumino* means "to enlighten" or "to illuminate." Throughout the rest of the homily, the same term is predominantly translated as "illuminate" on the basis of flow and context. Here, Origen quotes a biblical verse in which RSV employs the term "enlightens."

5. Jn 1.9.

6. The direct object to which Origen refers here is the true light.

7. Mal 3.20 (4.2).

8. Cf. Jb 18.5.

9. Manasseh: 7th-century B.C. king of Judah; see 2 Kgs 21. Ramses II (1301–1234 B.C.) is called Pharaoh at Is 30.2–5 and 36.6, and "Pharaoh" means "unjust and cruel," referring to Ex 1.8–14.

10. Uzziah is probably intended, rather than Ahaz. Ahaz (*Achaz*) was son of Jotham and grandson of Uzziah (*Ozias*), all kings of Judah (Uzziah's reign was 736–716 B.C.) and all wicked in the sight of the Lord according to Isaiah and 2 Chronicles 26-28. According to Is 1.1, the vision of Isaiah concerning Jerusalem and Judah occurred during these reigns. According to Is 6, however, the Lord gave Isaiah the commission and ability to speak prophecy only in the year when Uzziah died. In *Hom in Is* 1.1, Origen states that "Isaiah could not see a vision" as long as King Uzziah (*Ozias*) was alive. Here, in *Hom in Jgs* 1.1, Origen mentions that "Isaiah could not see a vision" during the time of "Ahaz (*Achaz*)." It is likely that Origen meant Uzziah and not Ahaz here in *Hom in Jgs* 1.1.

11. Is 6.1–3.   12. Cf. Eph 5.16.

of his [Jesus'] bodily presence? Hear what the prophet foretold about the days of our Lord Jesus Christ: "Justice will rise up in his days, as well as an abundance of peace, until, by reason of which, the moon should be no more."[13] So, if we accept this, that "the days" in which the Savior remained[14] on the earth were days "of justice" and "peace," then how will we explain that days "of justice" rose up for those who crucified him and who did not accept his coming and pledge faith in him? Or how will there seem to have been "an abundance of peace in his days" among those who handed him over to death by means of false accusations? How will days "of justice" and days "of peace" seem to have arisen for those in whose minds the darkness of injustice and rage dwelled? And, again, if what is written should refer to those days which the Savior lived out in the flesh—"Justice will rise up in his days, as well as an abundance of peace"—then, since the present days are not those days, consequently "his justice" does not rise up nor is "an abundance of the peace" of Christ found among the faithful and religious now. Rather, every single person acquires by virtue of his actions and way of life more "days" for himself either of injustice and war or "of justice" and "peace."[15]

In fact, listen to the prophet saying, "For those who fear my name, the sun of justice will rise up,"[16] so that, without doubt, he may make for them "days of justice," that is, "days of Jesus." Moreover, he says of the wicked that "the sun of justice" will set for them, without doubt for those in whom justice is asleep. In

---

13. Ps 71.7 (72.7). The term *extollatur* is from *extollo*, which means "to lift up" or "to put off" or "to defer." The nearest connotation here from the dictionary is "to put off," but the word in the passive is translated as "to be no more" for clarity in the English. The meaning is that the darkness will be lifted. (The Greek word in the LXX is *antanaireo*, which means "to cancel.") For all dictionary references, see C. T. Lewis and C. Short, *A Latin Dictionary* (Oxford: Clarendon Press, 1993).

14. The deponent verb here, *demoror*, means "to linger," "delay," or "remain alive," but the word is translated here as "remained" for clarity in the English.

15. Origen argues here that "days of justice" logically must refer to individuals and how they live their lives, rather than to one time period in human history versus another.

16. Mal 3.20 (4.2).

them and for them the darkness of injustice has risen up. But, similarly, do you want to learn from the prophet who they are who possess "an abundance of peace"? Hear how he says in the Psalms: There is "great peace for those who love your name, and there is no stumbling-block for them."[17] Therefore, "the days of justice and an abundance of peace will rise up for those who love the name of the Lord."

But even the impious possess their own light, from which without doubt "days of evil" rise up for them. Now, do you also want this to be proven to you from the Scriptures? Listen to what is written: It is said, "The just will always have light, but the light of the wicked will be extinguished."[18] You see, therefore, that the "light of the wicked" is a certain kind that "will be extinguished," but it is "the light of the just" that continues "into eternity." And I do not know if anyone believes so foolishly as to suppose that there is some essential light that may be said to be, on the one hand, "of the wicked" and, on the other hand, "of the just." That certainly cannot be in any way true. For the light of the world created by God is one,[19] which shines for all in common and equally.[20] But as we explained above, it is to be understood that our soul either is "illuminated by the true light"[21] that will never be "extinguished," that is, Christ, or, if that light does not possess in itself what is eternal, without doubt it [the soul] is illuminated by that temporary and extinguishable light, by that one "who transforms himself into an angel of light"[22]

17. Ps 118.165 (119.165).
18. Prv 13.9 and Jb 18.5–6.
19. The word "created" modifies "light," not "world," so that it is the light that is created by God.
20. Similarly, in *De principiis* 3.1.10 Origen stresses that God's grace rains down on everyone by one operation. This grace produces mercy or a hardening of the heart in each individual, according to that individual's own will. See *Origen: On First Principles,* trans. G. W. Butterworth (Gloucester, MA: Peter Smith, 1973; Torchbook edition), 172–74.
21. Cf. Jn 1.9
22. Cf. 2 Cor 11.14. The Latin term here for "transforms," *transfigurare,* not only means "to change in shape," "transform," "transfigure," and "metamorphose," but also "pretend to be" or "disguise oneself as someone else." Here Origen stresses that the Devil, the fallen angel of darkness, can change form in order to appear to human beings, by pretense, to be an "angel of light."

and illuminates the heart of the sinner with a false light, so that those lights that are present and transitory may seem to him to be good and very bright. By that light they are illuminated who say that pleasure is the greatest good.[23] By that light they are illuminated who search for wealth and worldly honors[24] and earthly glory, as if it is the age of eternity now.[25] Therefore, they also are "in the days" of his light that "will be extinguished" (for all the things that they do, desire, and long for will be extinguished). The heretics also are illuminated by this light, proclaiming "a knowledge falsely named."[26] Illuminated from this

23. Origen here refers to the Greek philosopher Epicurus (341–270 B.C.), who argued that one should strive in life for a state of pleasure, *ataraxia*, which can be achieved only by seeking prudence as the highest virtue. See Henri Crouzel, *Origène et la philosophie* (Paris: Aubier, 1962), 27–31; A. J. Festugière, *Épicure et ses dieux* (Paris: Presses universitaires de France, 1946; 2d ed., 1968; Eng. trans. C. W. Chilton, Oxford: Blackwell, 1955); and Norman Wentworth DeWitt, *Epicurus and His Philosophy* (Minneapolis: University of Minneapolis Press, 1954).

24. The Latin term for "worldly" here is *saeculi*, and the phrase may also read as "honors of the age."

25. This phrase, *quasi aeternitatis memoriam*, may read, "as if a memory or recollection or remembrance of eternity or immortality." Either way, Origen alludes to those who seek glory in this life as a means of achieving a feeling of immortality or eternal life now.

26. Cf. 1 Tm 6.20. Origen refers here generally to the various Christian Gnostic groups in his day who claimed to possess the true knowledge of reality and salvation. Origen found their dualistic views, which identified the material world with evil, and their elitist views, which restricted salvation to a privileged few, inconsistent with Christian doctrine as handed down from Jesus through the apostles. At places within his works, Origen states that his thought and faith are in opposition to those of Gnostic leaders such as Valentinus (c. 100–c. 175) and Basilides (c. 135–160), as well as another thinker of the early Church period, Marcion (c. 85–c. 160), who purported certain views similar to those of the various Gnostic groups. For example, see *De princ.* 2.9.5 (trans. Butterworth, 133). For texts attributed to Gnostic leaders, such as Valentinus and Basilides, or their followers, see *The Gnostic Scriptures*, trans. Bentley Layton (Garden City, NY: Doubleday and Company, Inc., 1987). A useful overview of Valentinian Christian Gnostic views is provided by a combined reading of *The Secret Book according to John* (or *Apocryphon of John*), *The Reality of the Rulers* (or *Hypostasis of the Archons*), *The Gospel of Truth*, and *Treatise on Resurrection (Epistle to Rheginos)*. See Layton, respectively, 23–51, 65–76, 250–64, and 316–24. For secondary treatments of Gnosticism and the early Church, see C. Markschies, *Gnosis: An Introduction*, trans. J. Bowden (London and New

source, Marcion calls the God of the Law just but not good.[27]

Accordingly, if we have understood correctly what are the days that are illuminated by our Lord Jesus Christ, "the true light," and what are the days that are illuminated by him "who transforms himself into an angel of light"[28] and whose light "will be extinguished," we also can properly understand those "days of Jesus" about which it is said that "the people served the Lord all the days of Jesus."[29] For it is certain that he who possesses in himself "the days of Jesus" "would serve the Lord." Nor can it happen that somebody, possessing in himself "the days of Jesus" and "the light" of Christ, would serve the Devil[30] or would

---

York: T & T Clark Ltd, 2003); Alastair H. B. Logan, *Gnostic Truth and Christian Heresy: A Study in the History of Gnosticism* (Edinburgh: T & T Clark Ltd, and Peabody, MA: Hendrickson Publishers, 1996); H. Strutwolf, *Gnosis als System. Zur Rezeption der valentinianischen Gnosis bei Origenes* (Göttingen: Vandenhoeck & Ruprecht, 1993); H. Jonas, *The Gnostic Religion*, 3d ed. (Boston: Beacon Press, 2001); A. LeBoulluec, *La notion d'hérésie dans la littérature grecque: II–III siècles*, Études Augustiniennes (Paris, 1985); K. Rudolph, *Gnosis: The Nature and History of Gnosticism*, trans. R. McL. Wilson (Edinburgh: T & T Clark Ltd, 1983); P. Perkins, *The Gnostic Dialogue: The Early Church and the Crisis of Gnosticism* (New York: Paulist Press, 1980); and R. M. Grant, *Gnosticism and Early Christianity*, 2d ed. (New York: Columbia University Press, 1966).

27. Marcion set himself apart from other Christian Gnostic schools of thought with views including the rejection of the god of the Old Testament as an evil demiurge who created the material world, setting him over against the benevolent God of Jesus represented by the few passages from Paul's letters and the Gospel of Luke that Marcion claimed were not tainted by the other, so-called apostles and their successors. For more on Marcion's thought, see Adolf von Harnack, *Marcion: The Gospel of the Alien God*, trans. John E. Steely and Lyle D. Bierma (Durham, NC: The Labyrinth Press, 1990; original German, Leipzig: J. C. Hinrichs'sche Buchhandlung, 1924); R. J. Hoffmann, *Marcion: On the Restitution of Christianity* (Chico, CA: Scholars Press, 1984); E. C. Blackman, *Marcion and his Influence* (London: SPCK, 1948); J. Knox, *Marcion and the New Testament: An Essay in the Early History of the Canon* (Chicago: University of Chicago Press, 1942); and R. S. Wilson, *Marcion: A Study of a Second Century Heretic* (London: Clarke, 1933).

28. Again, the verb *transfiguro*, translated here as "transforms," holds in this context the negative connotation of "disguises," referring to the deceptions of the Devil.

29. Jgs 2.7.

30. In some cases, as here, *Zabulus* is a Latin name for the Devil, in addition to *Satanus*, and is roughly transliterated from the Greek, Diabolos (*Zabu-*

serve avarice. Nor can it happen that someone would be illuminated by the light of truth and would serve falsehood. Nor can the one illuminated by the light of sanctification be devoted to lust and impurity. Indeed, even the Apostle declares as follows: "For what does justice share with injustice? Or what fellowship is there between light and darkness? Moreover, what agreement does Christ have with Belial? Or what does the believer share with the unbeliever?"[31]

Accordingly, let us pray that Christ, who is "the true light,"[32] may make good days in us always, and that we may never possess in ourselves—by the Devil illuminating us—"the evil days" about which the Apostle says, "Buying back time because the days are evil."[33] For we possess "evil days" when we search for carnal instead of spiritual things, earthly instead of heavenly things, transitory instead of eternal things, present instead of future things. When, therefore, you see that desires of this kind rise up in you, be assured that you are standing "in evil" and wicked "days." And indeed, for that reason, devote yourself to prayers so that you may be freed from "the evil day," and, just as the Apostle says, so that you may be snatched up out of "the present evil age."[34] For in the manner in which we spoke above, not only do the "days" become "evil," but also the "age" becomes "evil."

2. "Therefore, the people served the Lord all the days of Jesus and all the days of the elders who lived after Jesus."[35] Blessed is he who "in the days of Jesus serves the Lord," who is enlightened by his word and wisdom, who is illuminated by his com-

---

lus is the collateral form of the Greek word Diabolos). The Latin sometimes employs the term *Satanus* and at other times *Zabulus,* and this translation, while treating them as synonymous, tends to translate *Zabulus* into English as "the Devil" and *Satanus* as "Satan."

31. 2 Cor 6.14–15.
32. Jn 1.9.
33. Eph 5.16. The term here, *redimentes,* from *redimo,* has several possible meanings, including "to buy back," "ransom" or "redeem," "set free," "rescue," "purchase." RSV says "make the most of," and KJV says "redeeming." "Buying back" provides the appropriate connotation here.
34. Gal 1.4. The Latin term for "age" here is *saeculum.*
35. Jgs 2.7.

mands, who receives from his teaching the light of knowledge. Still, secondly, in addition to him, he also is blessed who "serves the Lord in the days of the elders who lived after Jesus." Are not "the elders" who "lived" either with Jesus or "after Jesus" none other than the apostles, who themselves also illuminate our hearts with their writings and precepts and make certain days in us from that light which they themselves, after coming, took as a share from "the true light"?[36] Accordingly, he who is illuminated and instructed by the precepts of the apostles and trained up by the apostolic examples to serve the Lord, he is the one who is said to "serve the Lord in the days of the elders who lived after Jesus." Moreover, do you wish to see why, just as the Savior "was the true light that enlightens every man coming into this world,"[37] the apostles also were "the light of the world"? In the Gospel it is written, with the Lord saying to them, "You are the light of the world."[38] Even now the apostles are "the light of the world." Without doubt through their precepts and mandates they illuminate for us the "days" in which "we are to serve the Lord."

3. And, moreover, he said: "All the days of the elders who lived longer days after Jesus."[39] This does not seem to me casually mentioned, that "the ancients"[40] or those "of longer days"[41] are said to be "the elders who lived after Jesus." Indeed, it is for God alone to know who "after Jesus" would have lived among "the elders," who would have made "a longer day," that is, who would have emitted from himself the greater light, whether Paul or Peter, Bartholomew or John. Nevertheless, the saints are called "those of longer days." But, on the contrary, at that time, when the world will be filled up with temptations, when, "with injustice increasing, the love of many will grow cold,"[42] and when "the Son of man comes, he will have difficulty finding faith upon the earth,"[43] at that time, it is not said that they are

---

36. Jn 1.9.
37. Ibid.
38. Mt 5.14.
39. Jgs 2.7.
40. The Latin term here for "ancients" or "ones of great age" is *longaevi* from the adjective *longaevus-a-um,* and is used here as a substantive.
41. Origen asks here which is meant in the Bible by the term that in Latin is *longaevi:* "the ancients" or "those of longer days."
42. Mt 24.12.
43. Cf. Lk 18.8.

going to be "long" days, but, rather, they are said to be shorter, just as the Lord said, "If those days had not been cut short, not any flesh would be saved."[44] Therefore, the evil days are said "to be cut short," but "the ancients"[45] are the good days of much time[46] and, in a certain measure, of great length,[47] during which "we serve the Lord." Yet, see that he also pointed this out in the Gospel, that "For the elect those days will be cut short."[48] Thus, "for the elect the evil days," the days of injustice and temptation, "will be cut short." And, as I believe, when once "the evil days" have begun to be cut short for the elect, they are always cut short and diminished until they are reduced to nothing and completely fade out and utterly disappear. On account of these things, I think there was also that one who said: "Let that day disappear on which I was born."[49] So then "the evil days are cut short for the elect" and disappear, but the days of the holy elders are lasting[50] and long.

Moreover, that which occurs to us while talking—and hopefully it has occurred by the Lord's prompting—what he said is not to be omitted: "The people served the Lord all the days of Jesus."[51] He did not say "one" day has been of Jesus, but many are "the days of Jesus." Therefore, how many days do we count according to this order that we explained? I believe that in the same way one day of his is justice, another is sanctification, another is prudence, another is mercy, and likewise for every single good quality of the virtues they are counted as "the days of Jesus" during which "the Lord" is served, because by these virtues of the soul the Lord is pleased.[52] Indeed, patience also is

---

44. Mt 24.22.

45. Again, this term *longaevi* can also mean "the ones of great age" or "the long-lived ones."

46. Origen (and Rufinus as translator) likely means by "time" the number of days.

47. Origen (and Rufinus as translator) likely means the length of each day.

48. Mt 24.22.   49. Jb 3.3.

50. The term *longaevi* is an adjective here and means "ancient" but is translated here as "lasting" for clarity in English.

51. Jgs 2.7.

52. The Latin term Rufinus employs for "soul" here is *animus,* perhaps as a synonym for *anima,* but more specifically referring to the mind, or the ratio-

counted as a day of his, and gentleness and piety and goodness, and everything that pertains to a virtue you shall call a day of his. And so "during all the days of Jesus you will serve the Lord," that is, in all these virtues "you will serve the Lord."[53] For the instruction of holy Scripture does not wish that you should possess in yourself some aspects of these virtues and neglect others, but that, adorned in all these virtues and invested in the performance of them, "you may serve the Lord." Moreover, in the same way, someone also possesses "the days of the elders" in himself and "serves the Lord in their days,"[54] when he is fulfilling what the apostle Paul says: "Be imitators of me, as I also am of Christ."[55]

4. "In the days," it is said, "of those elders who knew all the works of the Lord."[56] Who is "he who knows all the works of the Lord," if not he who does them? Indeed, as it were, it was said of the sons of Eli that they were "sons of scorn,[57] knowing not the Lord,"[58] not that they were ignorant of the Lord—since they undoubtedly also were teachers to the rest—but because to such a degree they acted as those act who do not know the Lord. In this way also what it says here must be heard: "they who knew every work of the Lord." And not only is it said, "they knew the work of the Lord," but it added, "they who knew every work of the Lord," that is, they who "knew" the Lord's work of justice and sanctification and patience and gentleness and piety. And

---

nal part of the soul. For more on Origen's understanding of the nature and parts of the human soul, see Henri Crouzel, *Origen: The Life and Thought of the First Great Theologian,* trans. A. S. Worrall (San Francisco: Harper & Row, 1989), 88.

53. See the end of *Comm in Song* 1.5 for Origen's idea that each of the virtues is equal to Jesus himself. See *Origen: The Song of Songs Commentary and Homilies,* trans. R. P. Lawson, ACW 26, 84–90, esp. 89–90. For consideration of this idea within Origen's theology, see Elizabeth Ann Dively Lauro, *The Soul and Spirit of Scripture within Origen's Exegesis,* The Bible in Ancient Christianity 3 (Boston: Brill Academic Publishers, Inc., 2005), 229–31.

54. Cf. Jgs 2.7.

55. 1 Cor 4.16; cf. Phil 3.17.

56. Jgs 2.7.

57. The term here is *pestilentia,* which means "pestilence" or, in the poet Catullus, can mean "the scornful."

58. 1 Kgs 2.12 (1 Sm 2.12).

everything that comes from the commands of God is called "the work of the Lord." But just as it is the work of the Lord, the work of the Devil is without doubt contrary to it. For it is certain that, just as justice is the work of God, so also is injustice the work of the Devil, and, just as gentleness is the work of God, so also would anger or rage be the work of the Devil. Accordingly, they are said "to have known" the work of God who do his work.

Yet, since it becomes even clearer from the authority of the Scriptures in what manner Scripture may be accustomed to saying "to know" or "to know not," see how it is written also elsewhere. It is said, "He who heeds a command will not know an evil word."[59] Now, "he who heeds a command," can it happen that "he does not know evil words"? Indeed, he knows, but "to know not" is said because he guards against and avoids evil words. Moreover, what is said concerning the Lord and Savior himself is that "he did not know sin."[60] It is certain that "to have been ignorant of sin" is said because he did not do the work of sin. Therefore, in this way, he also is said "to know the works of the Lord" who does "the works of the Lord." Yet he is ignorant of the work of God who does not do the work of God.

5. Moreover, how do we pass over what it added: "those who knew the great works of the Lord that he did for Israel"?[61] What, indeed? Are there any small "works of the Lord" distinct from these ones that may be called "great"? I think that every work of God is indeed great. But, if they are compared to each other, the works of the Lord are said to be either great or small, according to the capacity of those to receive it, for whom the work is done. For example, he led the people of Israel out of Egypt "with a strong hand" and "with a raised-up arm."[62] Having tormented Egypt with prophetic, heavenly signs, "he made a way in the sea."[63] He gave manna to the people in the desert.[64] "From

---

59. Cf. Eccl 8.5.
60. Cf. 2 Cor 5.21.
61. Jgs 2.7.
62. Dt 5.15; cf. Ex 6.6 and 13.3. The Latin word *filios* can mean "sons" or "people," and this translation employs "people" in these homilies wherever Origen (or translator Rufinus) refers to Israel or to a foreign nation.
63. Cf. Ex 14.21.
64. Cf. Ex 16 and Wis 16.20.

the sky" he spoke to Moses.[65] He gave the Law written "upon stone tablets."[66] Are not these "great works of God"? But if you should compare to these things that work—that "God so loved this world that he gave his only Son"[67] for the salvation of the world—you will find that all those deeds are small compared to the greatness of this work, which even we also must know and believe. And we must be engaged in "the works of the Lord"[68] not carelessly, but faithfully and attentively, so that we also may be found to be "in the days of Jesus" Christ and "in the days of the elders," his holy apostles, with whom we also may deserve to receive participation in the heavenly inheritance, through our Lord Jesus Christ himself, "to whom are glory and dominion forever and ever. Amen."[69]

65. Cf. Ex 19.3.
66. Cf. Ex 24.12.
67. Jn 3.16.
68. Cf. Jn 6.28–29.
69. 1 Pt 4.11.

HOMILY TWO

On that which is written:
"And Jesus, son of Nun, servant of the Lord, died."[1]

NCE MORE THE death of Jesus has been read aloud to us. And he, indeed the "son of Nun," that he "died"[2] is not at all surprising. For he released to nature what was due. But because we had established that these things read about the son of Nun refer to our Lord Jesus Christ, it must be considered how it may fittingly be said also of that one: "Jesus died." Talking about this still according to the authority of Scripture, I think that in certain persons Jesus lives, but in certain persons he is "dead."[3] Jesus lives in Paul and in Peter and in all those who can justly say, "I live, but no longer I, but Christ lives in me."[4] And again he says,[5] "But to me to live is Christ and to die is gain."[6] Therefore, in those kinds of persons Jesus is justly said to live.

But in whom is "Jesus dead"? Without doubt, in those who, for instance, by often repenting and again committing sin, are said to insult the death of Jesus, about whom the Apostle, writing to the Hebrews, says, "Those crucifying again the Son of God within themselves and making a public spectacle of him."[7] Accordingly, you see that in sinners not only is "Jesus" said "to die," but also he is declared "crucified and mocked" by them. Moreover, reflect within yourself whether, when out of greed you plan and

---

1. Jgs 2.8. 2. Ibid.
3. For Origen's identification of the virtues with Jesus Christ, see *Hom in Jgs* 1.3 and *Comm in Song* 1.5 as well as Dively Lauro, *The Soul and Spirit of Scripture*, 195–237.
4. Gal 2.20. 5. Origen refers to Paul here.
6. Phil 1.21. 7. Heb 6.6.

desire to lay waste to another's goods, you can say that "Christ lives in me."[8] Or if you plan debauchery, if you are excited with anger, if you are inflamed with envy, if you are spurred on by jealousy, if you revel in drunkenness, if you are puffed up with pride, if you act with cruelty, in all these matters can you say that "Christ lives in me"? So, therefore, in this way, Christ "is dead" for sinners by virtue of the fact that in them nothing of justice is at work, nothing of patience, nothing of truth, and indeed nothing of all that is Christ.[9]

Whatsoever virtues are done by the saints, however, it is said that Christ is he who effects them, just as the Apostle also says, "I can do all things in him who greatly strengthens me, Christ."[10] Moreover, the Lord himself in the Gospels has given an excellent distinction about this, when he says, "Whosoever has confessed in me before men, I also will confess in him before my Father who is in heaven. But he who has denied me before men, I also will deny him before my Father."[11] You have seen that with regard to "those who confess," he has said, "confess in himself," as the one who himself lives in them and performs the works of life in them. But, in those "who deny" him, he did not preserve the same likeness of the word[12] such that he would say that he who would deny in me, I also will deny in him, but, rather, [he said,] "he who would deny me before men, I also will deny him before my Father," in order to show that he who "denies" is indeed outside of him [Jesus], but he who "confesses" is in him [Jesus]. On that account, therefore, here also Scripture says that when "Jesus had died, another generation arose after them who did not know Jesus and the works that he did for Israel."[13]

2. "And the people of Israel did evil before God."[14] God, Omnipotent Ruler,[15] ensure that it should never happen to us that

---

8. Gal 2.20.

9. Again, for Origen's identification of the virtues with Jesus Christ, see *Comm in Song* 1 and Dively Lauro, *The Soul and Spirit of Scripture*, 195–237.

10. Phil 4.13.

11. Mt 10.32–33.

12. That is, the preposition "in" occurs in the clauses concerning confession, but not in the clauses concerning denial.

13. Jgs 2.8 and 10. 14. Jgs 2.11.

15. In the Latin edition "Omnipotent Ruler" is not capitalized, but this translation of the homilies capitalizes nouns in the vocative in English.

Jesus Christ, after he has risen from the dead, again should die in us. For what does it profit me if in others he should live on account of virtue and in me should die on account of the weakness of sin? What does it profit me if he does not live in me and in my heart and if he does not complete the works of life in me? What does it profit me if on account of good desires, good faith, and good works by another he is nourished and restored, but because of evil thoughts and impious desires by me and in my heart, because of wicked desires, he is, in a certain manner, suffocated and killed?

For instance, see what Scripture adds, that: "Another generation," it is said, "arose, which did not know Jesus and the great works that he did."[16] That "generation that did not know" the Lord "Jesus" is that generation "of evil thoughts" and wicked desires that "proceeds[17] from the heart."[18] That is "the generation that does not know" the Lord "Jesus" nor "the great work that he did for Israel." You see that sinners always come to the point of forgetting[19] even that "great" and excellent "work that the Lord did," that he was crucified "for our sins and rose for our justification."[20] I believe that this is why the Apostle, fearing this forgetfulness, said to his disciple Timothy, whom he considered special: "You shall remember that Christ Jesus rose from the dead."[21] For he knew[22] that he could have forgotten[23] about this work so great, that "he rose from the dead," if a sinful generation were to rise up in the heart. Therefore, "another generation that did not know Jesus" or the elders[24] "did evil in the sight of the Lord."[25]

---

16. Jgs 2.10.
17. The subject that proceeds here is the "generation."
18. Cf. Mk 7.21.
19. The term here for "to forget" is *obliviscor*, which literally means "to lose from the memory."
20. Rom 4.25.
21. 2 Tm 2.8. Note that "the dead" here is plural.
22. The term here for "to know" is *scio*.
23. The term here for "to forget" is again from *obliviscor*.
24. The term here for "elders" is *presbyteri*, in contrast to the term used in *Hom in Jgs* 1 for "elders," which was *seniores*.
25. Jgs 2.10 and 11, and cf. Jgs 2.8.

3. "And this generation served the Baals," it is said, "and abandoned the Lord God of their fathers."[26] Indeed, the people of old did these things, but since these things were not written for them but are said "to have been written for us, for whom the ends of the ages have come,"[27] let us see whether in greater part these things seem to be said about us rather than about them. And do you wish to see that those things are explained to be about us not by me but by the Apostle? Listen to what he himself says: "But what does Scripture say in the case of Elijah, how he speaks against Israel to God? 'Lord, they have killed your prophets, they have demolished your high altars, and I alone have remained, and they seek my life.'[28] And indeed what does [Scripture] say is the divine reply to him? 'I have left as a remnant for myself seven thousand men who did not bow down to Baal,'"[29] and adds, "Therefore, in this way," he [the Apostle] says, "and at this time the remainder have been saved according to the election of grace."[30] You see, then, that he understands those who "bowed down to the Baals" to be among the multitude of nonbelievers, and those "who did not bow down" to be among the remnant of believers. And this shows that those unbelievers and impious persons who lived during the time of the Savior "bowed down to the Baals" and worshiped images, but these who believe and complete the works of faith "did not bow down to the Baals." For neither is it mentioned anywhere in the histories nor in the Gospels nor in any other Scriptures that anyone at the time of the Savior would have bowed down to images,[31] but this is said particularly about those who were kept bound, indeed as if shackled, by their sins. Whence it is certain that as often as we sin and "are taken captive under the law of sin,"[32] we "bow down to the Baals." But neither have we been called to this nor

---

26. Jgs 2.11–12.
27. Cf. 1 Cor 10.11.
28. The term here for "life" is *anima*.
29. Rom 11.2–4.
30. Rom 11.5.
31. The term here for "images" is *simulacra*, which can be translated also as "likenesses."
32. Cf. Rom 7.23.

have we believed in conformity with this, so that we again would serve sin and "bow down" before the Devil, but, rather, so that "we would bow down at the name of Jesus," since "at the name of Jesus every knee is bent in heaven and on earth and in the regions under the earth,"[33] and so that we "would bow down to the Father of our Lord Jesus Christ, from whom every family[34] in heaven and on earth is named."[35]

But what does it profit me if, coming to prayer, I "should bend the knees" of my body "to God" and yet I "should bend the knees" of my heart to the Devil? For if "I shall not have stood firm against the tricks of the Devil,"[36] I "have bent my knees" to the Devil. And if I shall not have "stood" firmly "against" anger, I "have bent my knees" to anger." And, similarly, if I shall not have firmly resisted lust, then I "have bent the knees" of my heart to lust. And in the case of every one of these single things that are contrary to God, I will seem to do this, just as those also did who "worshiped the Baals and abandoned the God of their fathers," who led them out of the land of Egypt,"[37] unless "I shall have stood" firmly and bravely. So then, let us not think that, because we seem not to worship images, these things therefore do not pertain also to any of us. What each man worships in preference to the rest, what he admires and loves above all other things, this is God to him. In short, this is what God requires from man before all and above all things by his command: "You shall love," it is said, "the Lord your God with your whole heart and your whole soul[38] and all your strength,"[39] desiring in a certain manner to master for himself[40] all the affections[41] of the

---

33. Phil 2.10.
34. The term here for "family" is *paternitas,* which literally means "the descendant of one's father."
35. Eph 3.14–15.
36. Cf. Eph 6.11.
37. Jgs 2.11–12. Cf. Ex 12.42.
38. The term for "soul" here is *anima.*
39. Dt 6.5.
40. The terms *praeoccupare* and *erga* literally mean "to take or seize upon to himself beforehand," but "to master in advance for himself" renders more clarity in English.
41. The term for "affection" here, *affectus,* most literally means "state or dis-

human mind[42] in advance, and knowing[43] that what someone "has loved with his whole heart" and "his whole soul[44] and his whole strength," this is God to him.

Let every single person now investigate himself and in secret examine what things from his heart may boil up the flame of love in him most of all and above all other things, which passion is cherished by him more eagerly than the rest. You yourselves shall make a judgment about these things. On the balance of your examination weigh these things, and, if there is something that weighs more on the scale of love, this is God to you. But I am afraid lest love of gold should weigh more with very many people, and the weight of greed should sink them down by a sufficiently suppressed scale. And to this person in particular it will be said: "You cannot serve God and mammon,"[45] that is, greed. I also fear lest in others the love of lust and pleasure should weigh so much more that he should sink all the way down to the ground, and in others the love of worldly glory and ambition for human rank should outweigh all things. And I strongly believe that there are few who, measuring their desires within themselves and weighing them equally in the balance, find that the weight of God's love outweighs all the other things, which are human. I know someone who had weighed these things within himself by the most complete examination and had found that all feelings that were inside of him were drawn into that part where the love of God was. Then he said with all confidence that, "Neither death nor life nor angels nor powers nor present things nor future things nor height nor depth nor another creature will be able to sepa-

---

position of mind," but can have a positive connotation, meaning, for example, "love" or "desire," or a negative connotation, as used by Seneca and Pliny, to mean "ignoble or low passion or desire." The use here seems neutral and not negative.

42. The term here for "mind," *mens,* refers generally to one's "reason," "intellect," or "discernment," but it can also be translated as "heart," "soul," or even "spirit." This translation of the homilies, however, generally renders it as "mind" in order to distinguish it from the Latin term *animus,* which is translated as "spirit," and *anima,* which is translated as "soul," unless otherwise noted.

43. The term here for "knowing" is *sciens* from *scio.*

44. The term here for "soul" is *anima.*

45. Mt 6.24.

rate us from the love of God, which is in Christ Jesus our Lord."⁴⁶ But this is Paul who was able to say these things in this manner, because "neither present things nor future things nor another creature can separate" him "from the love of God."

O, would that we also now could say this, too: that neither gold nor silver nor fleshly desire nor worldly glory and transitory and temporal rank or bodily allurements nor regard for children or spouse "will be able to separate us from the love of God." Certainly let this, too, be said by us confidently: that neither the love of secular literature nor the false conclusions of philosophers nor the deceptions of astrologers and the feigned directions of the stars nor the contrived predictions by the surreptitious trick of the demons nor any love wholly of foreknowledge sought after by illicit means "will be able to separate us from the love of God, which is in Christ Jesus."

Moreover, did not the error of all paganism⁴⁷ receive a beginning from the fact that men want those things which they love much to be gods and they ascribe a divine name to each of the human vices and desires? For those burning with desire for money and love of greed, they call the god of that desire Mammon—as with the Syrians. The lovers of lust and pleasure designate for themselves Venus as the goddess of this vice by which they are excited. Similarly also, for the rest of the vices they made into a god for themselves the very passion by which they are driven. Whence even the Apostle says the same thing; namely, he says: "and greed, because it is the worship of idols."⁴⁸ Therefore, you see that not only to worship an image⁴⁹ but also to strive after "greed" is considered to be "worship" and servitude "to idols." Therefore, in this way, we also, since we are so dedicated to some vices that we "love" them "with the whole heart and the whole soul and all strength," we are said to worship idols and "to have gone after foreign gods."⁵⁰

---

46. Rom 8.38–39.
47. The term here, *gentilitatis*, is from *gentilitas*, which can be translated also as "heathenism."
48. Col 3.5.
49. Again, the term here for "image" is *simulacrum*.
50. Cf. Jgs 2.12.

4. "And they worshiped," it is said, "alien gods, the gods of the peoples who were around them, and they incited the Lord to anger."[51] See how great are the effects of sins, so that by sinning we are said to provoke to wrath the one [God] in whom not only is there no feeling[52] of anger but not even indeed any other passible movement. But, he [God] remains unchangeable in his nature, nor is he ever thrown into feelings of anger. I, however, inflict anger upon myself through those sins that I commit, just as the Apostle himself says these things, teaching: "But, according to your hardness and unrepentant heart you store up," it is said, "for yourself anger on the day of anger and of the revelation of God's just judgment, who will render to each person according to his works."[53]

5. Therefore, "they provoked the Lord to wrath and abandoned the Lord, and they worshiped Baal and Ashtaroth. And the Lord grew angry with rage against Israel and handed them over into the hands of plunderers."[54] As long as someone serves God, he is not "handed over into the hands of plunderers." When, however, he "has abandoned the Lord" and has begun to serve his passions,[55] then it is said of him that "God handed them over into disgraceful passions," and, again, "He handed them over to a false mind,[56] so that they do those things which are not fitting."[57] Why? Because, it is said, "they have been filled with every wickedness, wretchedness, fornication, greed"[58] and all the rest which are mentioned, just as here now also it is said that because "they served and worshiped the Baals and Ashtaroth, God handed them over into the hands of plunderers, and it was done at the hands of their enemies."[59]

Consequently, as I already have often said, the Jews read these things as if they are stories of things accomplished and

---

51. Jgs 2.12.
52. The term here for "feeling" is *affectus*.
53. Rom 2.5–6.
54. Jgs 2.12–14.
55. The term here for "passions" is *passionibus*.
56. The term here for "mind" is *sensus*, which can refer more specifically to any of the faculties of perceiving, feeling, or understanding.
57. Rom 1.26 and 28.   58. Rom 1.29.
59. Jgs 2.13–14.

past. "We," however, "for whom these things written"[60] are mentioned, must know that, if we have sinned against the Lord and we worship as God the pleasures of our minds[61] and the desires of the flesh, then we also again are handed over and given over into the hands of the Devil according to apostolic authority. In fact, listen to this exact saying about him who had sinned: "I handed over," it is said, "such a man to Satan for the destruction of the flesh so that the spirit may be saved."[62] Therefore, you see that, even now, not only through his apostles has God "handed over" sinners "into the hands of enemies," but also through those who preside over the Church and have the power not only to loose but also to bind sinners "they are handed over for the destruction of the flesh" when on account of their transgressions they are separated from the body of Christ.[63]

And, as it seems to me, in a double way even now men are handed over from the Church into the power of the Devil, in this way which we said above, when his transgression is made visible to the Church and he is banished from the Church by the priests so that, branded with infamy by men, he may feel ashamed and, when he has been converted, that which follows may happen to him: "that the spirit[64] may be saved in the day of our Lord Jesus Christ."[65] Yet, in another way, someone is "handed over to the Devil," when his sin is not made manifest to men, but God "who sees in secret,"[66] looking into his mind and inclinations[67] and seeing that they serve vices and passions, and looking into his heart and seeing that [God] is not worshiped, but rather greed or lust or boasting or other such things, that kind

60. Cf. 1 Cor 10.11.
61. The term for "minds" here is *animi* from *animus*. See n. 64, below.
62. 1 Cor 5.5.
63. Cf. Mt 16.19.
64. The term here for "spirit" is *animus*, which also can mean "the intellectual faculty in the soul," "the mind," or even "the seat of the will." This translation of homilies usually translates this term as "spirit," and on occasion as "mind," in contrast to *anima*, which it translates usually as "soul" and on occasion as "life." This is significant since Origen views the human soul and spirit to be two separate parts of the human person.
65. 1 Cor 5.5.
66. Mt 6.4 and 6.
67. The term here for "inclinations" is *animos* from *animus*.

of person the Lord himself "hands over to Satan." How does he "hand" him "over to Satan"? He [God] departs from his mind and turns away and flees from his evil thoughts and shameful desires and abandons the "empty house" of his heart.[68] And then that which is written will be fulfilled in that man: "But when an impure spirit has gone out from a man, he travels around dry places; and, if he has not found rest, he returns to his home; and, finding it empty and clean, he takes with him seven other spirits more vile than himself, and, entering in, he dwells in that house; and then the final state of that man will become worse than the first."[69]

Therefore, in this way God is to be understood "to hand over" those whom he hands over, not that he himself would hand over anyone, but on account of the fact that he deserts unworthy persons, namely, those who do not so improve themselves and cleanse themselves from sins that God may live gladly in them. When he [God] flees and turns himself away from a soul[70] that is standing in impurity and vices, the soul is said to be handed over from him because it is found to be empty of God and seized by a vile spirit. And for that reason let us be vigilant with the greatest zeal and hasten to cleanse ourselves from vices and evil desires so that we may keep God within us and so that he may deign to dwell in us, as long as he takes delight in our actions and words and thoughts, if we do all that we do according to his will, so that "whether we eat or we drink, or whatever else we do, we may do all things in the name of" our "Lord"[71] Jesus Christ, "to whom are glory and dominion forever and ever. Amen."[72]

68. Cf. Mt 12.44.
69. Mt 12.43–45.
70. The term here for "soul" is *anima*.
71. 1 Cor 10.31.
72. 1 Pt 4.11.

HOMILY THREE

On the fact that the people of Israel were handed over "into the hands of enemies"[1] *and about Othniel and Ehud*

WHEN "THE PEOPLE of Israel did evil in the sight of God, and they forgot[2] the Lord their God," and, abandoning him, "they served the Baals and the wooden idols"[3] of the foreign nations, "at that time storing up wrath for themselves," "they were handed over" by the just judgment of God[4] "into the hands of enemies"[5] according to these things which the present reading has declared, "into the hands," it is said, "of Cushanrishathaim, king of Mesopotamia."[6] Now, "Cushanrishathaim" means "their humiliation." Accordingly, "they were handed over into the hands" of him who would humiliate them. Also, because they themselves acted impiously at the tops of the mountains[7] against the Most High, for that reason they are handed over by him into humiliation.

But I do not wish that you should think that this divine providence was only for the people of old, [that is,] that he would hand over to be humiliated those who were exalted impiously and that they would be healed by the salutary medical practice of "opposites by means of opposites," but that God does not administer this kind of providential health upon his Church now.[8]

---

1. Cf. Jgs 2.14.
2. The term here for "forgot" is *obliti sunt* from *obliviscor;* see *Hom in Jgs* 2, n. 19.
3. Jgs 3.7. An even more literal rendition of the term here, *lucus,* is "sacred woods or woods sacred to a deity."
4. Cf. Rom 2.5.   5. Cf. Jgs 2.14.
6. Jgs 3.8.
7. Cf. 4 Kgs 17.10 (2 Kgs 17.10); Jer 2.20.
8. An even more literal rendition of this phrase is as follows: "but that now providential health of this kind is missing from the omnipotent God in re-

Even now it is "Cushanrishathaim, king of Mesopotamia," to whom are handed over the souls to be humiliated and stricken down, who, out of contempt for Christian humility, gave themselves over to pride and arrogance. The vice of pride is quite hateful in the sight of God, because, as Scripture says: "Pride is the beginning of separating from God,"[9] and again elsewhere Scripture says: "God opposes the proud, but he gives grace to the humble."[10] Therefore, if someone—despising the humility of Christ, who for us, "although he was God, became man and humbled himself all the way to death"[11]—is raised up and elevated, he rushes toward the powers and dignified ranks of the age, strives after the skills by which these things are obtained, even if they are against faith and religion, and he neither flees nor trembles so long as he may obtain what he desires. Thereafter it happens that "he does evil in the sight of the Lord,"[12] and, after he has obtained the highest marks of [these worldly] powers and he has ascended to the very greatest heights of pride, then, cast down from there, he is handed over to this "Cushanrishathaim," namely, to one from "the princes on high"[13]—just as at one time the Pharaoh[14] and at another time Hiram[15]—since [God] may humble the person who had been exalted excessively, so that he may weaken him and wear him out till at length he comes back to his senses and searches for the Lord. For, when he was fixed in pride and self-exaltation, he did not know God.[16]

2. Now, then, these persons who are handed over on account of sin and placed in tribulation, let us see what they do. Indeed, this is what is written: "And they cried out to the Lord when they were being oppressed, and he freed them from their exi-

---

spect to his Church." The phrasing in the text above, however, renders more clarity to the English. Origen will go on to stress that God cares in this way for the people of the present day as much as God did for the people of old.

9. Sir 10.12.
10. 1 Pt 5.5, quoting Prv 3.34.
11. Cf. Phil 2.6–8.
12. Cf. Jgs 3.7.
13. Cf. Eph 2.2.
14. Cf. Ex 1.11.
15. Cf. 3 Kgs 9.11 (1 Kgs 9.11). Hiram was the king of Tyre.
16. The term here for "did not know" is from *ignorare,* which can mean to choose to "ignore" or "pay no attention to" or "disregard." See Origen's use of this and similar terms to stress human intention and responsibility also in *Hom in Jgs* 1.4.

HOMILY THREE

gent circumstances. And he led them out from darkness and the shadow of death, and he broke off their chains."[17] Moreover, each one of us, even if he is small, even if he is very small, even if he is of no value in secular terms, he can labor under the vice of pride; and nothing is so foul and detestable, as Scripture says, as "a proud pauper and a lying rich man."[18] But sometimes that disease of pride not only penetrates the common paupers but also strikes even the priestly and levitical order itself. Now and then you may even find among us some people who have been set forth as an example of humility and arranged in a circle around the altars as certain mirrors for those looking on, in whom the vice of arrogance stinks, and, from the altar of the Lord, which needed to burn with the sweetness of incense, the most foul odor of pride and self-exaltation beams forth. But that most foul odor should be cast off—for heaven's sake!—from this entire holy Church and especially from these ones who serve in holy places, so that we may, as Paul said, be able to be made into "the good fragrance[19] of Christ,"[20] "lest perchance the Lord should become angry"[21] and "we should provoke the holy one of Israel to anger"[22] and "he should hand" us "over into the hands of Cushanrishathaim," so that we may learn, in the tribulation of our reproof, the humility that we have needed to teach in the knowledge of Christ.[23]

But see the benevolent Lord mixing mercy with severity and weighing the degree of his punishment according to the balance of justice and mercy. He did not hand over transgressors for all time, but for as much time as, it is said, they served the Baals, for that much time "they" also "are slaves of Cushanrishathaim," that is, "for eight years."[24] Learn this also, you,

17. Ps 106.6 and 14 (107.6 and 14).
18. Sir 25.2.
19. The word for "fragrance" here is *odor*, which is the same word translated above as "foul odor."
20. 2 Cor 2.15. Cf. *Hom in Song* 2.6 and *Comm in Song* 1.2.
21. Cf. Ps 2.12 (2.11).
22. Cf. Is 1.4.
23. Notice that Origen is addressing other clergy or Church leaders and teachers of the faith here.
24. Jgs 3.8.

O Listener, whoever you are, who are conscious of any error of your own. And however much time you know yourself to have been in error, for however much time you have done wrong, by that much time, no less, humble yourself to God and you shall give him satisfaction in the confession of repentance. Do not wait so that Cushanrishathaim humbles you and necessity forces repentance against your will, but, on your own, anticipate the hands of that tormentor, because, if you yourself have corrected your ways, if you have reformed yourself, God is "benevolent and merciful,"[25] who may mitigate punishment for the one who anticipates it by repenting.

Moreover, let us also consider this: that so long as "they were serving Cushanrishathaim," they who had been handed over on account of sins and were not "crying out to the Lord," no one was raised up who could save them. But when "they did cry out to the Lord, then the Lord raised up a savior for Israel, and he saved them."[26]

3. And indeed Scripture speaks of the savior Othniel, whose name means "the time of God for myself." Accordingly, those first people were pulled out of humiliating enslavement by this Othniel, and peace was restored to the people, which the pride and diverse crimes[27] of the community drove away a short time previously. Truly, since we said that it is possible for King Cushanrishathaim to be understood, in some spiritual sense, as both one of the enemies and "a leader of the powers of the air,"[28] so it also seems to me to follow logically that Othniel, who was raised up in order to liberate the people, is someone from "the heavenly host"[29] and the archangelic troops that "are sent to the aid of those who receive the inheritance of salvation."[30] And they are savior-angels who are represented in the outward figure either of Othniel or Ehud, because, as we often have shown, not only

---

25. Cf. Sir 2.11.
26. Jgs 3.9.
27. The term for "crimes" here, *facinora*, most literally means "deeds," "acts," or "actions," but can have a distinct negative connotation.
28. Cf. Eph 2.2.
29. Cf. Lk 2.13.
30. Cf. Heb 1.14.

are we attacked by contrary powers, but also divine and good powers are sent to our aid by the Lord.[31] Nevertheless, let us see who that Othniel would have been, of what family, of what nobility. "Son," it is said, "of Kenaz, brother of Caleb,"[32] of that laudable and admirable man, Caleb, who was a companion and associate of Jesus son of Nun, about whom, as we were able, we have discussed on those occasions which have seemed fitting.[33]

Accordingly, what does Scripture say about that Othniel? Afterwards it said that: "The people of Israel cried out to the Lord,"[34] then, "the Spirit of the Lord came upon Othniel, and he judged Israel."[35] Do you suppose someone is among us who "may let out a cry to the Lord" that is so strong and so just that it is worthy to be heard, and the people may be worthy to receive a judge, and such a judge whom "the Spirit of God" would fill so that he would be able to maintain a just judgment? And indeed for that reason this very book is called "Judges," and in it are described the judges who have judged the people.

For just as the other books are called "Kings" or "Kingships" in which it is described how each of the kings ruled and what he did, so also in this little book the deeds of the judges are recorded, and not only is it described whether anything was accomplished by them justly and beneficially, but also whether anything was committed negligently. Nevertheless, for that reason, it was described both ways, if you desire to know, so that the present leaders and judges of the Church, discerning those things which were done by them laudably, may follow the previous examples. If, however, in some way they are at fault in those things, may they be on guard and turn away [from those previous examples]. Consequently, great praise for this first judge Othniel is reported, that "the Spirit of God came over him" and through the Spirit of God "he judged Israel,"[36] which I scarcely remember as having been said about any other [judge]. Accord-

---

31. For Origen's angelology, see "Angels," Johan Leemans, *The Westminster Handbook to Origen*, ed. John Anthony McGuckin, and *De principiis* 1.8.1. Cf. *Hom in Nm* 11.4.
32. Jgs 3.9.
33. Cf. *Hom in Jos* 18 and 20.3–6.
34. Jgs 3.9.
35. Jgs 3.10.
36. Ibid.

ingly, there are also today among all the churches that are under the sky a great many judges by whom judgment has been given not only concerning deeds but also concerning souls.[37] But I do not know whether there is any such judge of the Church whom "God" considers worthy "to fill with his Spirit," so that, as Othniel himself was honored by the testimony of Scripture, those [leaders] for whom we desire this may also merit the testimony of God. Therefore, it says: "And the Spirit of the Lord came over him, and he judged Israel. And he went out to war, and the Lord handed over King Cushanrishathaim into his hands."[38] Why in this way? Because "the Spirit of the Lord" was in him and "his hand was greatly strengthened over Cushanrishathaim."[39] And after these things it says that: "The land was tranquil under this judge for forty years."[40] You see how abundant is divine mercy. "For eight years the people of Israel had been slaves"[41] on account of the sins of many, and "for forty years"[42] they continue in peace on account of the justice of one.

4. But what is said after these things? "And," it is said, "Othniel, son of Kenaz, died."[43] I see a dangerous thing. "Othniel died." Why? Because the people who were keeping such a judge were now unworthy. In fact, in the following, it tells about the time of his death: "And," it is said, "the people of Israel did further evil in the sight of the Lord, and the Lord greatly strengthened Eglon, king of Moab, against Israel."[44] Observe that, because they were now unworthy to keep such a leader, for that reason a good judge is taken away from them. And because "they did evil in the sight of the Lord, Eglon, king of Moab," a wicked enemy, is raised up against them.

You see that our sins supply forces to our enemies, and, when we "do evil in the sight of the Lord" and we transgress, then our adversaries "are greatly strengthened by the Lord" and forces are given to hostile people. If you examine this according to the letter, you will find that enemies would not become strong un-

---

37. The term for "souls" here is from *anima*.
38. Jgs 3.10.
39. Ibid.
40. Cf. Jgs 3.11.
41. Cf. Jgs 3.8.
42. Jgs 3.11.
43. Ibid.
44. Jgs 3.12.

less our sins were to confer forces upon them. Or, if you consider according to spiritual meanings that, similarly, contrary powers could not become strong against us nor could the Devil himself prevail in anything against us unless we were to supply forces to him by our vices, then he would be exceedingly weak against us unless we were to make him strong by sinning and unless through our sins he were to find in us a place to enter into and have dominion. For that reason, even the Apostle forewarns us, saying: "Refuse to give place[45] to the Devil,"[46] just as also here now we read that, after "the people of Israel did evil in the sight of the Lord," they "gave place to the Devil."[47] For "the Lord greatly strengthened Eglon, king of Moab, and he joined to him all the people of the Ammonites and the Amalekites."[48] Not only, it is said, was "he" himself "greatly strengthened" by the sins of the people of Israel, but to him are joined wretched allies "from among the people of the Ammonites and Amalekites" who together with him would attack Israel.

5. "And," it is said, "the people of Israel served Eglon, king of Moab, for eighteen years."[49] Notice that the divine Scripture indicates also the measures of punishment: there it says "eight years"[50] and here "eighteen years." Now, it is certain that the durations of punishment are determined according to the measure of sin and the delay of our conversion. For also those "eighteen years" of slavery passed, and it is not reported that [during that time] "they cried out to the Lord" or that they were turned from their wickedness. But it is again said that after eighteen years, "The people of Israel cried out to the Lord, and the Lord raised up for them a savior, Ehud, son of Gera, son of Benjamin, an ambidextrous man."[51] Behold what kind of man that one is who is raised up in order to save Israel. He has nothing "left" in himself, but he has a right hand on both sides; for this is what is called "ambidextrous." He is truly a worthy leader of the people and judge of the Church who would do nothing "left,"

---

45. Origen (and Rufinus as translator) means to emphasize physical space. The Latin term is *locus*, which can also be translated as "room" or "space."
46. Eph 4.27.
47. Jgs 3.12; cf. Eph 4.27.
48. Jgs 3.12–13.
49. Jgs 3.14.
50. Jgs 3.8.
51. Jgs 3.15.

whose "left hand does not know what the right hand is doing."[52] On both sides he is "right"; in faith he is "right," in deeds he is "right." He possesses nothing from those who are placed "to the left,"[53] to whom it is said: "Depart from me, workers of iniquity, I do not know you; go into the eternal fire, which God has prepared for the Devil and his angels."[54] And if it is permissible to assume such things by comparison, I think that, according to a spiritual understanding, all the saints also should be called "ambidextrous," and, to the contrary, the Devil and his princes, if it is possible to say, are called "ambi-left." For what they do is wholly "left," wholly perverse, wholly destined to eternal fire with those who are "to the left."

6. But let us see what this "ambidextrous" judge does. It is said, "The people of Israel sent gifts to Eglon, king of the Moabites, by the hand of Ehud, and Ehud made for himself a two-edged sword, the length of [his] extended palm, and he girded it to his right thigh."[55] You see that everything that "Ehud, this ambidextrous one," does is "right." He is right both in the hands and in the feet. For he carries the sword on the right thigh so that he may come to "the king of Moab" and kill him. We had said above that those whom God is said to raise up for the salvation of the people and to free the people of Israel, that is, saviors or judges, may bear the image of some leaders from "the heavenly host"[56] and the powers on high whom God may send out to the aid of those who have cried out to him with their whole heart and who have, through the conversion of repentance, turned divine mercy toward themselves.

But lest this seem to us to be taken for granted by the audience, we must confirm it in accordance with the authority of the Scriptures. It is written in Exodus that our fathers, the people of Israel, when they had served the Egyptians and the very harsh king Pharaoh for a long time in the production "of clay and brick,"[57] it is said, "they cried out to the Lord,"[58] so that God himself would say: "The cry of the people of Israel has risen up

52. Cf. Mt 6.3.
53. Cf. Mt 25.33.
54. Cf. Mt 25.41 and Lk 13.27.
55. Cf. Jgs 3.15–16.
56. Cf. Lk 2.13.
57. Cf. Ex 1.14.
58. Ex 2.23.

HOMILY THREE

to me."⁵⁹ And indeed, by having sent out Moses, he [God] visibly led them out. Moreover, Scripture reports that a destroyer angel was sent who indeed would destroy all the firstborn of Egypt but would touch none of the Israelites.⁶⁰ And so it is declared to have been a heavenly power that led out the people from the yoke of slavery away from the devastated and overthrown Egyptians. A similar thing is reported in the histories, [namely,] that under the king of the Assyrians, Sennacherib, "an angel of the Lord" is sent who would free the city from siege and the people from imminent annihilation, with "185,000"⁶¹ of the enemies slain and destroyed after one night.

So, therefore, even now, according to the same reasoning, we must pay attention so that, whenever we are handed over into captivity on account of our sins, "we should cry out to the Lord." But let us cry out not by mouth but by mind,⁶² so that the sorrow of our heart "may produce a fountain of tears from the eyes,"⁶³ just as he who said, "Throughout every single night I will wash my bed; I will moisten my blanket with my tears."⁶⁴ If, thus, we are converted from evil ways so that we do not touch evil things any longer; if, thus, we cease from pride so that there is no longer any pride, so that we may have a taste for nothing arrogant,⁶⁵ then the Lord will send to us also his heavenly power by which we will be freed from the yoke of satanic slavery. And this power may effect for us all things right and beneficial, which make us abandon "the left way which leads to destruction"⁶⁶ and call us back to the true "way," to him who says, "I am the way and the truth and the life,"⁶⁷ Christ Jesus our Lord, "to whom are glory and dominion forever and ever. Amen."⁶⁸

---

59. Ex 3.9.   60. Cf. Ex 11.4 and 12.21–30.
61. Cf. 4 Kgs 19.35 (2 Kgs 19.35).
62. The term for "mind" here is *mente* from *mens*, which also means "intellect," "thought," or "intention," and therefore connotes the orientation of the mind.
63. Cf. Sir 22.19 and Jer 8.23 (9.1).   64. Ps 6.7. (6.6).
65. The term here for "to have a taste of" is *sapio*, which can also mean "to know," with the connotation of "being experienced with."
66. Cf. Mt 7.13.   67. Jn 14.6.
68. 1 Pt 4.11.

HOMILY FOUR

On Shamgar and Jabin and Sisera

THE REIGN OF the ambidextrous Ehud is followed by the reign of Shamgar.¹ But let us see how Ehud, whose name means "praise," ended his reign. History has taught us what things were written about King Eglon, how this Ehud, most wise, by a certain cunning and, so I might say, by a shrewdly but laudably deceptive practice, killed the tyrant Eglon,² whose name means a "whirling round"³ or "of orbits."⁴ Therefore, it is proper that such judges are also from among our people, as was that Ehud, whose name means "praise," since they would cut off all the spinning motions and orbits of the evil path and would slay the king of the Midianites.⁵ Moreover, "Midianites" means "flux"⁶ or "rushing out."⁷ Consequently, what leader or ruler can be perceived or understood to be over this lax and dissolute people other than the word of that philosophy which judges pleasure to be the greatest good,⁸ which pleasure

---

1. Cf. Jgs 3.31. 2. Cf. Jgs 3.17–25.

3. The term here for "whirling around," *rotatus*, can also be translated as a "turning."

4. The term here for "orbit," *orbita*, can also be translated as "track" or "rut," as in a wheel rut, or "a circuit."

5. Eglon is the king of the Moabites. See *Hom in Jgs* 3.4–6 and Jgs 3.12–30. Here, for comparison, Origen refers to Gideon's defeat of the Midianites in Jgs 7.

6. The term here for "flux," *fluxus*, can also be translated as "flowing" or "flow."

7. The term here for "rushing out," *effusio*, can also be translated as "a pouring forth" or "violent movement," and can have the connotation of "excess" or "extravagance" or "exuberance of spirits."

8. Origen refers here to the Epicurean philosophy, which posited the highest good as pleasure, to be attained by cultivating prudence as the highest virtue. See *Hom in Jgs* 1.1 n. 23 on Epicureanism.

HOMILY FOUR 71

the evangelical word—which is compared to a "sword"[9]—kills and destroys? And the prophetic word itself should be closed up in their stomach and also in the lowest part of the entrails[10] by the arguments of an ambidextrous teacher, so that, closing them up by the declaration of the truth, he may extinguish every "meaning" of a depraved philosophical doctrine and crass understanding, "which meaning elevates itself and raises itself up against the spiritual knowledge of Christ,"[11] so that, by doing these things and fighting by means of the word of God, every single judge of the Church may himself also become a praiseworthy Ehud, about whom the Lord may say: "Well done, good and faithful servant, you have been faithful over a little; I will set you over much."[12]

2. But yet, having recalled to ourselves briefly those things from the previous reading, that is, about the end of Ehud, let us now see what kind of beginning also Shamgar had, whose name means "foreigner there."[13] For it is true that all who are men of God are foreigners in this world and foreign residents on earth, as also he who said, "I am a foreign resident among you on earth and a sojourner, just like all my fathers."[14] Therefore, the Holy Spirit also calls this Shamgar a foreign resident there, that is to say, here. For that which is "there" for the Holy Spirit, who is in heaven, is "here" for us. What, then, is said of Shamgar? It is said, "He struck down the Philistines, 600 in number, with a plough-handle"—or—"the foot of a plough."[15] I see in regard to Shamgar another kind of praiseworthiness: he fights with a "plough." Ehud fought with a sword, but this one with a plough. Yet, here he also conquers, he overcomes and destroys the Philistines. Therefore, it can happen that a judge of the Church may not always brandish a sword, that is to say, he may not always use the harshness of a word and sharpness of a reproof, but

9. Cf. Heb 4.12.
10. For the way in which Ehud killed Eglon, see Jgs 3.17–22.
11. Cf. 2 Cor 10.5.
12. Mt 25.21.

13. The term here for "foreigner," *advena,* can also be translated as "stranger" or "alien" and can also have the connotation of "ignorant," "unskilled," or "inexperienced."

14. Ps 38.13 (39.12b).   15. Jgs 3.31.

sometimes he may even imitate the farmer and, furrowing the land of the soul as if with a plough and breaking it open more often by a gentle admonition, he may make it suitable for receiving seeds. Therefore, when we do not use arguments and sharpness against enemies but we drive away vices and sins from the souls of hearers with a coarse and simple admonition, they also will be killed in the same way as the Philistines.

Moreover, you yourself, O Disciple,[16] shall be the ploughman of your soul, so use this plough that Shamgar uses. But when "you have put your hand to the plough," do not "look back,"[17] that is to say, after "you have taken up your cross and followed Christ,"[18] after you have renounced the world[19] and these things of the world, do not "look back," do not again seek after those things that "you had counted as dung on account of Christ,"[20] because, if you always held "the hand" to that "plough," then you could say confidently, "But, far be it from me to glory except in the cross of our Lord Jesus Christ, through whom the world has been crucified to me and I to the world,"[21] and say these words to yourself: "Ten thousand will fall to your right and a thousand to your left, but they will not draw near to you."[22]

Moreover, this thing itself that he said, "Shamgar killed Philistines in the 600s,"[23] does not seem to me casually said. For what need was there to point out the number also? Unless perhaps with this very number those things are more clearly indicated about which we spoke earlier. For the senary number,[24] which when multiplied reaches into the 600s, contains a figure of this world, which it is said was completed in six days. Therefore, it is said, "he struck down six hundred with a plough," he to whom "by the cross of Christ the world has been crucified."[25]

16. The term here for "disciple," *auditor,* can be translated as "pupil," "listener" or "hearer," or "reader."
17. Cf. Lk 9.62.
18. Cf. Mt 16.24.
19. The term here for "world," *saeculum,* can also be translated as "age."
20. Cf. Phil 3.8. 21. Gal 6.14.
22. Ps 90.7 (91.7). 23. Cf. Jgs 3.31.
24. Cf. *Hom in Lv* 13.5.1.
25. Cf. Gal 6.14. Note that Origen here presents the cross of Christ as the plough that strikes down worldly men.

3. But what is added after these words? "And," it is said, "the people of Israel did further evil in the sight of the Lord, and Ehud died."[26] In these words this observation also is surely made, which we pointed out earlier, that the good leader of the people dies on account of the sins of the people.[27] For since they have become unworthy and "have done evil in the sight of God," the man of God will be taken away from them.

But perhaps our people say: when is the Church of God without a judge? Even if the first has departed, another is summoned. Perhaps we will say something boldly, yet we say what has been written. The leader of the people and judge of the Church is not always given by God's decision, but proportionately as our merits demand. If our actions are evil and "we are engaged in evil in the sight of God," leaders are given to us according to our heart. And this I will demonstrate to you from the Scriptures. For hear what the Lord says: "They appointed a king for themselves and yet not by me, and a leader and yet not by my counsel."[28] And this statement, it seems, is about that Saul whom the Lord himself had chosen especially and had ordered to be made king. But, since he had been chosen not according to the will of God but according to the merit of a sinful people, he [God] denies that he [Saul] has been established with his [God's] will and counsel.[29]

Therefore, let us understand that some such thing has happened also in the churches, that either, according to the merits of the people in word and deed, a powerful ruler is assigned by God to the church, or, if "the people do evil in the sight of the Lord,"[30] to the church such a judge is given under whom the people suffer "hunger and thirst," "not hunger for bread or thirst for water, but hunger for hearing the word of God."[31] Therefore, let us so act and let us so pray lest divine indignation should ever condemn us to a "famine of the word" and to "thirst for the word," lest he should ever be taken away from us who would instruct us in word and deed, who, in character and in-

---

26. Jgs 4.1.
27. See *Hom in Jgs* 3.4.
28. Hos 8.4.
29. Cf. 1 Kgs 8–11 (1 Sm 8–11).
30. Cf. Jgs 4.1.
31. Am 8.11.

tegrity, would offer himself as a perfect example of patience and gentleness to the people. For if "we were to do evil in the sight of the Lord,"[32] that is, if we were to live wickedly, if we do our will and not the will of God, "Ehud dies" also for us, and Shamgar is taken away, and our glory will be rendered invisible, and "we will be handed over into the hands of Jabin, king of Canaan."[33] Now, "Jabin" means "understanding"[34] or "prudence."[35] Therefore, if we "did not esteem it fitting to hold to the knowledge of God, God hands us over to a false understanding, filled," it is said, "with injustice, wickedness, fornication, greed; full of envy, murders, contentiousness, deceit; gossips, disparagers, haters of God, insulting, proud, boastful, disobedient to parents, disordered, without good will, without compassion."[36] You see who and of what kind they are who "are handed over to a false understanding," who "are handed over to Jabin, leader of the Canaanites."[37]

4. "And the leader," it is said, "of Jabin's army was Sisera, and he himself lived among the people in Haroshethhagoiim, and there were in his possession 900 chariots of iron. And the people of Israel cried out to the Lord."[38] Even in this present matter the observation that we pointed out earlier is similarly maintained, that "the people of Israel" do not know "to cry out to the Lord" until after "they have been handed over into the hands of Jabin" or after they have been tormented by "Sisera, the leader" of his "army," in whose possession "there were," it is said, "900 chariots of iron,"[39] by which evidently "the stiff-necked people" were overthrown."[40]

Now, "Sisera" means "vision[41] of the horse." For that one is

32. Cf. Jgs 4.1.
33. Cf. Jgs 4.2.
34. The term, *sensus,* translated as "understanding" throughout this paragraph, can refer to a cognitive, affective, or moral mindset.
35. Cf. *Hom in Jos* 14.2 and 15.3.
36. Rom 1.28–31.
37. Cf. Jgs 4.2.
38. Cf. Jgs 4.2–3.
39. Jgs 4.3.
40. Cf. Ex 32.9.
41. The term here for "vision," *visio,* can also refer to a mental image.

"animal"⁴² and not "spiritual"⁴³ who does not see except those things that are of "the animal." That is his vision, and it is always his view.⁴⁴ And for that reason "the animal man" and "he who is according to the flesh"⁴⁵ always "persecutes him who is according to the spirit,"⁴⁶ while "the spiritual one" understands and "examines all things"⁴⁷ and understands from whom help for him is to be earnestly requested,⁴⁸ and "he cries out to the Lord,"⁴⁹ until for that soul which "has cried out to the Lord," prophecy,⁵⁰ which is in the figure of Deborah, is raised up,⁵¹ and, according to the grace and wisdom of prophecy, either the people of the Church are governed or likewise the understanding of every single mind and soul is directed,⁵² by Christ Jesus our Lord, "to whom are glory and dominion forever and ever. Amen."⁵³

42. The term here for "animal," *animalis,* can also be translated as "unspiritual" or "soul-like." Its translation as "soul-like" is specific in Christian thought to the terminology of Valentinian Gnosticism concerning the three types of people in this world. One type of people consists of spirits who are sparks of light trapped in this material world. Another is soul-like creatures who might be able to rise up to the light and be saved. And the third type is those who are empty and a part of the darkness of this material world. For Valentinian theology, see *The Gnostic Scriptures,* trans. Bentley Layton (Garden City, NY: Doubleday & Company, Inc., 1987). If Origen is playing on Valentinian terminology to describe Sisera, it is not a compliment. He is placing Sisera squarely outside the group of the Christian faithful and within the group of worldly men who deliberately ignore God and the virtues, which are God's attributes.
43. Cf. 1 Cor 2.14–15.
44. The term here for "view," *intuitus,* can also be translated as "a look" or (in the ablative singular) "respect" or "consideration."
45. The Latin term here is *caro.*
46. Cf. Gal 4.29.
47. Cf. 1 Cor 2.15.
48. Cf. Ps 120.1–2 (121.1–2).
49. Cf. Jgs 4.3.
50. Cf. Dt 18.15.
51. Cf. Jgs 4.4.
52. The term for "mind" here is *mens,* and the term for "soul" is *anima.*
53. 1 Pt 4.11.

HOMILY FIVE

On Deborah and Barak and Jael and Sisera

WE PASS FROM inquiries to inquiries and from mysteries to mysteries, and, when with difficulty and much effort we explain certain first things, difficult ones are followed by even more difficult ones, and they do not need the eloquence of human talent so much as they require the breath of divine grace. For without doubt the hearer will search, because of the sentence of the Apostle Paul that says: "All Scripture is divinely inspired and useful for teaching, for reproving, and for instruction in righteousness."[1] What that Scripture contains in itself, which without doubt we acknowledge to be itself divinely inspired, it may yield to us "for teaching," "for reproof," "for discipline," "for righteousness." For what is conferred on us from this if we read this which has been recited, that is, that "Deborah," it is said, "the woman prophetess," "wife of Lappidoth, herself was judging Israel at that time, and," it is said, "Deborah herself used to sit under the palm tree between Ramah and Bethel, on Mount Ephraim, and the people of Israel used to go up to her for judgment"?[2] Then what do these things which follow confer on us of knowledge or doctrine or righteousness either concerning Barak or Jael or even Sisera, "the commander of Jabin's army"?[3]

2. Accordingly, let us see whether perhaps by these things, just as also from the rest of the Scriptures, we may be taught something worthwhile about the more secret mysteries.[4] In the

---

1. 2 Tm 3.16.   2. Jgs 4.4–5.
3. Cf. Jgs 4.2.
4. Origen refers to the higher senses of meaning, the psychic (soul's) and the pneumatic (spiritual), non-literal meanings. For elaboration, see Introduction as well as Dively Lauro, *The Soul and Spirit of Scripture*.

first place, this very thing, that although a very great number of judges in Israel are reported to have been men, about none of them is it said that he was a "prophet" except "Deborah, a woman."[5] And in this, even the first aspect of the letter itself[6] renders to the female sex not a small consolation, for it invites women to avoid despairing in any way on account of the weakness of their sex,[7] for even they themselves can become capable of prophetic grace, and indeed they may understand and believe that the purity of mind, not the difference of their gender, merits this grace. But let us also see what aspect of the interior sense breathes forth a mystery. "Deborah" means "bee" or "speech." But indeed also in the passages above we said that Deborah is to be received in the form of a prophecy, which is a bee.[8] For it is certain that every prophecy produces the sweet honeycombs of heavenly teaching and the sweet honey of the Divine Word. Whence also David sang, saying, "How sweet your words to my throat, more than honey and the honeycomb to my mouth."[9] And again elsewhere he says, "The judgments of God are more precious than gold and any stone precious beyond measure, and sweeter than honey and the honeycomb."[10]

3. Moreover, let us consider that place where it is said that prophecy[11] "sits"[12] and where her place is described to be. "Under

5. Cf. Jgs 4.4.
6. Origen refers here to the literal or historical level of meaning of scriptural text as opposed to the higher, non-literal levels of meaning, the psychic (soul's) and pneumatic (spiritual) meanings. Again, for comparisons and distinctions, see Dively Lauro, *The Soul and Spirit of Scripture*.
7. Cf. *Hom in Jgs* 9.1.   8. Cf. *Hom in Song* 1.1.
9. Ps 118.103 (119.103).   10. Ps 18.10–11 (19.9–10).
11. In this homily translator Rufinus refers to Deborah not as prophetess (*prophetissa*) or as prophet (*propheta*) but as prophecy (*prophetia*). Rufinus is likely reflecting Origen's own turn of words in the original Greek by which Origen makes Deborah a representation of God's own word. Through Deborah's song about Barak, Jael, and Sisera (Jgs 5), God foretells, by means of allegory (indeed, a pneumatic meaning in Scripture), that, because the Church and not the Jews believe in Christ, God gives primacy to the Church and makes it not only the first to receive salvation but also the necessary vehicle by which to attain it.
12. The Latin term here for "sits," *residere*, also means "resides" or "dwells," but "sits" is better here to be consistent with the corresponding references below to Jesus sitting at the right hand of God in heaven.

the palm tree," it is said, "halfway between Ramah and Bethel."[13] Prophecy has a seat "under the palm tree" because "the righteous," David says, "will flourish as a palm tree"[14] for this reason: that prophecy leads the one taught by her instructions to "the palm tree of the high calling of God in Christ Jesus our Lord."[15] Moreover, she is said "to sit[16] halfway between Ramah and Bethel." "Ramah" means "the heights," while, on the other hand, "Bethel" means "the house of God." Observe in what places "prophecy" is said to "sit": between the heights and the house of God. For nothing low, nothing dejected, nothing of low value can be found in regard to the seat of prophecy; just as also Solomon no less, describing the seat of wisdom, says about wisdom that either "she herself stands at the gates of the cities" or she dwells "at the fortifications of the walls" or she "speaks freely" on high towers.[17] Therefore, in this way prophecy, which is represented now in Deborah, is said to dwell[18] between the house of God and the heights. For it does not teach us "to search for what things are above the earth, but rather for what things are in the heavens and on high, where Christ is sitting at the right hand of God";[19] to that place prophecy exhorts us to ascend, to that place she endeavors to place her disciples.

4. Therefore, first of all, this woman, it is said, "sent for and summoned Barak to herself."[20] Now, "Barak" means "a flash." Truly a flash is that which indeed holds light, but not a permanent light, for it shines brightly for a modicum of time and ceases. Therefore, this Barak seems to me to assume the figure of the first people, who first of all were called by prophecy and invited to hear the words of God and receive the gifts of the divine law, who indeed shone brightly and flashed for a brief time in the splendor of the law but did not endure for a long time, nor could they maintain the continuous brightness of the light. Therefore, as Deborah had said to Barak, that is, prophecy to

13. Jgs 4.5.
14. Ps 91.13 (92.12).
15. Cf. Phil 3.14.
16. The Latin term here for "to sit," *sedere,* could also mean "reside" or "dwell."
17. Cf. Prv 1.20–21 and Prv 8.1–3 and 9.3.
18. The Latin term here for "dwell" is *habitare.*
19. Cf. Col 3.1–2.
20. Jgs 4.6.

the first people: "And the Lord God of Israel has commanded you: 'Go up to Mount Tabor and take 10,000 men,'"[21] and the rest of the things that are written. Let us see what Barak, in the person of the people, replied to prophecy. He said, "I will not go up unless you also go up with me, because I know not the day when the Lord will send his angel with me."[22] Therefore, you see how prophecy communicated the words of God to those first people and says to them that the commands are given so that "they may ascend into the mountain," but they plead and say: "I will not go up unless you also go up with me."

And it is indeed true concerning the excuse, but it is false concerning the counter-promise. For it is certain that they did not ascend the mountain of God, but their promise to be ready to go up themselves with prophecy is false. For they did not follow prophecy to the point of believing in him about whom all prophecy has been written down: Christ. On that account, therefore, Deborah says to him, "I will go with you. Yet, know that your primacy will not be on this road which you walk, but into the hand of a woman the Lord will hand over Sisera."[23] Clearly it shows that "there will not be" among that people "primacy," nor will the palm of victory remain among them, "but into the hand of a woman," whose name is Jael, "Sisera will be handed over." Moreover, it is recorded that, while, according to the admonition of Deborah, that is, prophecy, Barak was pursuing the leader of the Philistines, Sisera, he [Barak] himself indeed was not able to seize him [Sisera], but the foreign woman, Jael, met him [Sisera] while he was fleeing. This woman [Jael] previously had had a pact of friendship with him [Sisera], and toward her he had made a turn [in his path of flight] for the sake of hiding and asked earnestly that he might drink water, but from her he was given milk to drink. And after she had placed him [Sisera] in hiding and had covered him up in skins, she fixed a stake, driven with a hammer, through his cheekbones, or jaws. And then upon meeting Barak, the one pursuing Sisera, she [Jael] showed Barak the already dead and prostrate Sisera.[24]

5. What of mystery, then, does all of this historical text reveal

21. Ibid.
22. Jgs 4.8.
23. Jgs 4.9.
24. Cf. Jgs 4.14–22.

to us? That foreign woman, Jael, about whom prophecy spoke when saying that victory would be accomplished "at the hand of a woman,"[25] contains the figure of the Church, which was assembled together from foreign peoples. Now, "Jael" means "ascent," because in fact there is no other ascent by which one may be raised up to heaven except "through the Church of the manifold wisdom of God."[26]

Therefore, she [Jael] is that very one who, while she ascends from bodily to spiritual things and from earthly to heavenly things, kills Sisera, who, we already said above,[27] contains the figure of fleshly vices and "animal"[28] man or man "formed from dust,"[29] because "Sisera" means "vision of the horse," about which Scripture says: "Do not become like a horse or a mule, in which there is no intelligence."[30] Therefore, she kills him with a stake; that is, she throws him down to the ground with the sharp point and power of the wood of the cross.[31] And not without reason is it recorded that with the stake she pierced through his jaws.[32] For that mouth which spoke of fleshly things and spoke of that doctrine which preferred the glory of the flesh, which persuaded the sages of this age to live in allurements and pleasure,[33] and had deceived humankind with the flattery of excess, that mouth, I say, is stabbed and pierced through with the wood of the cross, because the philosophy[34] had publically proclaimed

---

25. Jgs 4.9.

26. Cf. Eph 3.10. See also *Hom in Jos* 3.4–5, in which Origen refers to Rahab, the prostitute of Jericho, as a type of the Church and emphasizes that salvation is attained only within the Church.

27. *Hom in Jgs* 4.4.

28. The Latin term here is *animalis*. See *Hom in Jgs* 4.4, n. 42, above, and n. 46, below.

29. Cf. 1 Cor 15.48–49 and 2.14. Cf. *Hom in Jgs* 4.4.

30. Ps 31.9 (32.9). The Latin term here is *intellectus*, which can also be translated as "intellect" or "understanding."

31. The Latin term here for "throws down to the ground," *prosterno*, can also be translated as "makes him prostrate."

32. Cf. Jgs 4.21.

33. Origen refers here to the Epicurean philosophy which leads its followers to strive for a state of pleasure by seeking prudence as the highest virtue. See *Hom in Jgs* 1.1, n. 23.

34. Again, "the philosophy" is the Epicurean philosophy.

that "road" of pleasure to be "broad and wide" while Christ shows us that this "road" of salvation is "narrow and confined."[35] In this way, then, Jael, the Church, having concealed Sisera, the prince of vices, with skins, that is, having put him to sleep by the death of his members, handed him over to eternal slumber.

Yet, after this, Jael, the Church, "went out to meet" also the first people [Barak], who were pursuing Sisera. For Israel pursued "the law of righteousness, but did not arrive at the law."[36] Therefore, the Church "goes out to meet" even that one [Barak/the Jews (the first people)] and "shows" him her work; she shows him the accomplished victory and invites him into alliance for having overthrown the enemies.[37] For this is true what the Apostle says will happen "at the end time": "when the full number of the gentiles has entered in, then all Israel will be saved."[38] Therefore, "primacy" is indeed brought about "at the hand of" a foreign "woman";[39] nevertheless, even Barak is not excluded from a participation in glory, he who indeed had begun as the first but arrived at the end as the last. On the contrary, until he arrives, Jael, the foreign woman, snatches a victory in a certain manner while escaping notice.

The same figure went before also in the brothers Esau and Jacob.[40] For while Esau pursues wild beasts, while he waits in the ravines, Jacob, going before, and, nonetheless, on the counsels of a woman [his mother Rebecca], offering to his father [Isaac] prepared foods, received the blessing of primogeniture.[41] So also in the Gospel while the Lord is going out in order to raise up the daughter of the leader of the synagogue, a "woman," coming before, "who suffered a flow of blood," is the first to obtain health by the touch of faith.[42]

35. Cf. Mt 7.13–14.
36. Cf. Rom 9.31.
37. Cf. Jgs 4.22.
38. Cf. Rom 11.25–26.
39. Cf. Jgs 4.9.
40. See Origen's representation of Jacob and Esau as the Church and the Synagogue in *Hom in Gn* 12.
41. Cf. Gn 27.5–29. The Latin term for "primogeniture," *primitivatus*, also means "the firstborn."
42. Cf. Mt 9.18–26, Mk 5.21–43, and Lk 8.40–56. This refers to the woman with the hemorrhage whom Jesus healed. The woman's bleeding made her impure under Jewish law, yet Jesus touched her anyway in order to heal her. Af-

6. But if, likewise, something seems to attentive listeners to need explaining, why it is said he [Sisera] "drank milk," after he had requested water,[43] let us see whether perhaps according to mystical and allegorical rules some such thing can be revealed also about this. The nourishment "of milk" is, it is said in the holy Scriptures, this first moral instruction which is handed on to beginners as if to "young children."[44] For, in the beginning, instruction concerning the profound and more hidden mysteries is not to be taught immediately to the pupils, but the correction of morals, the amendment of discipline, and the first elements of religious life and simple faith are taught to them. That is the "milk" of the Church; these first elements are for "the young children" just beginning [in the faith].

But that food gives life and health to those indeed who have the intention of advancing toward the good, but to those to whom contrary things are pleasing, for whom there are in the heart extravagance, lust, greed, and all the impieties, a teaching of that kind offers death and destruction. So, therefore, it happens that by these and the same foods by which the good people are nourished, the evil people are suffocated, and in the way that it is life to the pious it then is death to the impious. In fact, as an example, the thing that we say may be made more clear: wine benefits the healthy and those living rightly, and, just as Scripture says, "the heart of a man"—of the healthy man at least—"[wine] delights,"[45] but to those ill with fever, if they were to take it, it brings forth ruin immediately and death. Thus it happens that the same thing taken in the same way should confer life indeed on one, but death on another. In this way, therefore, it is necessary to understand also that Sisera, that "animal

---

ter healing her, Jesus went to the daughter of the head of the synagogue and raised her up from an unconscious state. For Origen here, the woman with the hemorrhage represents the Church, who is given first place over the Jews, represented by the daughter of the head of the synagogue, because of her ready faith in Jesus Christ.

43. Cf. Jgs 4.19.
44. Cf. 1 Cor 3.1–2.
45. Ps 103.15 (104.15).

man"⁴⁶ and prince of vices, was destroyed by the teaching of the Church, which he did not receive in faith.

Moreover, each soul may advance enough with that evangelical and apostolic milk to put the Sisera in itself to sleep and to kill him. For if by these things the one fully instructed who "has put to death his members which are earthly: greed, fornication,"⁴⁷ and the others that the holy Apostle enumerates, has, it will seem, killed the Sisera in himself, let him show not only that these things are accomplished in the person of the Church, but also that each one is fulfilled in his soul. Therefore, because, as we said, Sisera indeed began to be pursued by the first people [Barak], yet was murdered by a woman [Jael], this Church of the gentiles,⁴⁸ and into her hand the palm of victory was given, at the consummation of all things, that is, at the end of the age, again the song will be sung to the Lord by Deborah, in which "primacy" indeed will be given to Jael, the Church of the gentiles, yet will not be silenced concerning the glorious action of Barak,⁴⁹ but the one reward of victory will be given both to the first and to the last,⁵⁰ through Jesus Christ our Lord, "to whom are glory and dominion forever and ever. Amen."⁵¹

---

46. Cf. 1 Cor 2.14. The Latin term *animalis* also means "unspiritual" or "soul-like."
47. Cf. Col 3.5.
48. The Latin term *gentium* means "foreigners" or "gentiles."
49. Cf. Jgs 5.6–15.   50. Cf. Lk 13.30.
51. 1 Pt 4.11.

HOMILY SIX

On the song which Deborah sang

SISERA, WITH his army and "war-chariots of iron," with which he attacked the people of God, was overcome. What prophecy foretold through Deborah was going to occur in this way.[1] And after victory was accomplished "at the hand of a woman [Jael],"[2] Deborah, it is recorded, sang that song as praise for the victory itself. But if we remember those things that were said above,[3] according to the mystical type—what figure there may be with respect to Deborah, also what there may be with respect to Barak, what sort of image the woman Jael may possess, who single-handedly killed the enemy of God's people, what image also there may be with respect to that very Sisera who was overthrown by the foreign woman with the power of wood—we understand all these mysteries to be those things which in the last times and at the end of the age are accomplished through the Church, and in this song it is recorded, as in her songs of victory, that is, the praise of victory,[4] about this time, namely, when "the last enemy, death, will be destroyed."[5] For then Deborah will rejoice exceedingly, that is, the glory of prophecy[6] will be made clear, because what she predicted has

---

1. Cf. Jgs 4.3 and Jgs 5. 2. Cf. Jgs 4.9.
3. Cf. *Hom in Jgs* 4.4–5 and 5.4–6.
4. Deborah sings of Jael's victory in Jgs 5.24–27.
5. Cf. 1 Cor 15.26.
6. As in homily 5, Rufinus here refers to Deborah as "prophecy"(*prophetia*) rather than "prophetess" (*prophetissa*) or "prophet" (*propheta*), and he likely carries on this method from Origen's intention in the original Greek to present Deborah as a representation of God's word, and thus her song of Jael, Barak,

been fulfilled. Then Jael, the Church, will conquer the enemy common to everyone, and, "after the full number of gentiles has entered in," then also Barak, that is, the "remnant of Israel, will be saved"[7] and will be received into the fellowship of victory. Accordingly, then, if we have become worthy, we also will sing that song filled with mystical and prophetic mysteries from which, because there is no time to examine all in detail—for the Church audience loves brevity—we will try nevertheless, either by examining a few of its first principles or by choosing ornaments here and there from it, to convey some encouragement to the hearers or to practice and meditate on those things among ourselves, so that we may become capable of singing again and again the song of Deborah.[8]

2. "For establishing leaders in Israel, with the willingness of the people, bless the Lord."[9] The blessing, it is said, by which "we bless the Lord" is "at the beginning about the leaders in Israel," and then afterwards "about the consent of the people." For example, when at first we begin to come to the worship of God, when we receive the beginning of the word of God and of the heavenly doctrine from "the leaders of Israel," those first principles[10] ought to be grasped eagerly by us. Yet, "the leaders of Israel," that is, of the Christian people, are to be understood, I think, as "the angels" whom the Lord appoints to attend to every least person in the Church, who also are said "to see always the face of the Father, who is in heaven."[11] These very ones, therefore, are the leaders, and from them we are to obtain the first principles.[12] For example, if some boy should go to lectures,

---

and Sisera as an allegory, indeed a pneumatic reading, stressing that God gives first place to the Church over the Jews because of the former's belief in Jesus Christ, thus making the Church the vehicle by which salvation is attained. See *Hom in Jgs* 5.3, n. 11.

7. Cf. Rom 11.25–26.   8. Cf. *Hom in Song* 1.1.
9. Jgs 5.2.
10. The term here for "first principles" is *initia*, which can also mean "beginning," "constituent parts," or "elements," or even "secret sacred rites" or "sacred mysteries."
11. Mt 18.10. For Origen on angels as guardians see *De principiis* 1.8.1.
12. 1 Cor 3.1–2.

he indeed is received by the teacher[13] and is made the pupil[14] of that instructor,[15] but he does not undertake the beginning of learning from that teacher[16] all at once, but, when he has received from him only the first principles,[17] he is handed over to be instructed by others, as thus I might say, to the leaders of the school itself, so that, after he has been instructed thoroughly by them, [and has received] as much as is in them, and after he has stored up the first principles[18] with them, then at length he may receive also the more perfect lessons of the Teacher himself.[19]

So, therefore, also now recalling the beginnings of our education, prophecy says that after we have begun at the hands of "the leaders," or after "the leaders" have begun to work in us, after that we may henceforth imitate voluntarily and with purpose and in this way come to an increase in improvements in order to bless now the Lord himself. But see what it says: "For establishing leaders in Israel,"[20] it is said. The beginnings are what are said "to be aided" by "the leaders"; but it is necessary to strive after these things now according to [our] own will and purpose so that [we] may be worthy to bless the Lord. For the people of Israel also, when they began to leave Egypt and cross the Red Sea, nothing was accomplished by means of their own labor, but everything through the leaders, that is, by the angels.[21] In fact, in this way Moses also says to the people: "You all," he says, "will be quiet, and the Lord will fight for you."[22] Or is not the destroyer

---

13. The term for "teacher" here is *magister*, which carries a connotation of strong authority.

14. The term for "pupil" here, *discipulus*, implies voluntary study rather than the learning required of a schoolchild.

15. The term for "instructor" here is *doctor*.

16. The term for "teacher" here is *praeceptor*, which can also be translated as "commander."

17. The term here for "first principles" is *prima elementa*.

18. The term here for "first principles" is *rudimenta*.

19. Origen seems to suggest here that the human soul receives various instructors in the faith, but the ultimate teacher, or *doctor*, is Christ himself. All preparation is in order for the soul to receive direct instruction from Christ. Therefore, in the English the term "teacher" is capitalized.

20. Jgs 5.2.
21. Cf. Ex 14.19.
22. Cf. Ex 14.14.

angel described as having fought on behalf of them openly[23]—the one indeed who killed the firstborn of the Egyptians—and in fact made the sheep of the Israelites not even bleat?[24]

It is not, however, always to be expected that the angels "should fight for us," but only "for establishing," that is, in our beginnings, we are helped by the angel-"leaders." For the rest, in the course of time, it is necessary also that we ourselves march out armed for battles. To be sure, before we may learn to recognize the battles, before we may consider fighting the battles of the Lord, we are raised up by the angel-"leaders." Before we may obtain the yearly provision of "heavenly bread"[25] and may be satisfied by the flesh "of the unblemished lamb,"[26] before we may become intoxicated with the blood of the "true vine"[27] which has risen up from the root of David,[28] so long as we are "babes" and are nourished "with milk"[29] and hold to discourse about the first principles of Christ, we act just as "babes under the angel-'overseers' and angel-'stewards.'"[30] But listen to how, as soon as we have tasted[31] the mysteries "of the heavenly host"[32] and have been restored by "the bread of life,"[33] we are incited to battle by the apostolic war-trumpet. For Paul, with a powerful voice, calls out to us, saying: "Put on the armor of God, so that you may stand firm against the tricks of the Devil."[34] He does not permit us to be concealed any longer under the wings of those giving the nourishment of milk. Instead, he summons us to the fields of combat. It is said, "Put on the breastplate of love"[35] and "receive" no less "the helmet of salvation,"[36] and, moreover, "the sword of the Spirit"[37] and, above all, "the shield of faith on

---

23. Cf. *Hom in Jgs* 3.6.
24. Cf. Ex 12.23–29 and 11.7.
25. Cf. Jn 6.51.
26. Cf. 1 Pt 1.19.
27. Cf. Jn 15.1.
28. Cf. Is 11.1 and Mt 1.6 and 20.
29. Cf. 1 Cor 3.1–2 and Heb 5.12–6.1.
30. Cf. Gal 4.2.
31. The term here for "tasted" is *gusto,* which has the connotation of "taking a little of" something.
32. Cf. Lk 2.13.
33. Cf. Jn 6.35.
34. Eph 6.11.
35. Cf. 1 Thes 5.8 and Eph 6.14.
36. Cf. 1 Thes 5.8 and Eph 6.17.
37. Eph 6.17.

which you may be able," he says, "to extinguish all the fiery darts of the evil one."[38]

Therefore, you see how all things happen in relation to the people of God by means of order and nothing confused; nothing disordered or distorted is carried out. "For at the beginning the leaders" help, but, when you have been aided and instructed by the leaders, then of your own accord and free will do those things which you learned from the leaders. And truly we are rightly committed to our will because of ripened beginnings and stored-up first principles, so that either our glory by right may be what is obtained by our virtue, or our guilt by law may be what comes by means of our idleness. For reason of these things, this is written: "For establishing leaders in Israel, with the willingness of the people, bless the Lord."[39]

3. But after these things it says: "Hear, Kings, and give ear, Governors: to the Lord I will sing, I will sing psalms to the God of Israel."[40] "Hear, Kings," it is said. It names "kings" those who assemble in order to hear the word of God. Rejoice exceedingly, O People of God, hearing the marks of your nobility. You are summoned to hear the word of God, and not as common people, but you are summoned as a king. For to you it is said: "Royal, priestly race, people claimed."[41] Therefore, because you are kings, deservedly our King the Lord Christ is called "King of kings and Lord of lords."[42] But just as you all have rejoiced exceedingly about the title of your nobility, so you must learn what each of you must do to become a king. Now, let me explain to you briefly in the following way. He makes you king over all things, if Christ reigns in you; for by reigning one is called "king." If, therefore, the spirit[43] reigns in you and the body submits, if you cast desires of the flesh under the yoke of the com-

---

38. Cf. Eph 6.16.
39. Jgs 5.2.
40. Jgs 5.3. The Latin verb *psallam* can mean "I will sing psalms" or "I will play a stringed instrument."
41. 1 Pt 2.9.
42. Rv 19.16.
43. The term here for "spirit" is *animus,* which can also be translated as "the mind," or rational part of the soul.

mandment, if you suppress the nations of vices with the tighter reins of your sobriety, deservedly you will be called a king, you who would be made new to rule yourself rightly.[44] Therefore, when you have been made such, fittingly as a king you will be summoned to hear the divine words.

But this which follows indicates something more bodily:[45] "Give ear, all you Governors."[46] For just as the governor is inferior to the king, so also, it seems, is giving ear inferior to hearing. For to hear pertains to the interior man, just as even the Lord said, "He who has ears for hearing, let him hear."[47] But to give ear tends toward exterior and bodily hearing. For this reason, then, here also those who must hear are called "kings," but those who must give ear are called "governors."[48]

"I will sing to the Lord, I will sing psalms to the God of Israel."[49] They are blessed who can "sing a song to the Lord." When we return to the Scriptures, we find many songs mandated in the holy books. We have an entire book written about the Song of Songs. Behold also in this book of Judges we have a song,[50] and in Numbers a song is written,[51] and in Deuteronomy[52] and in Exodus[53] and in the first book of Kings,[54] also in the first book of Chronicles,[55] and in many other places you will find

---

44. Here Origen highlights his tripartite anthropology of the human person and how the three parts—spirit, soul, and body—work either harmoniously under the direction of the spirit or in disharmony and confusion under the direction of the fleshly tendencies of the body. Origen also presents this same anthropology in *De principiis* 3.4, *Hom in Lv* 2.2.7, and *Hom in Lk* 11.3. For discussion, see Dively Lauro, *The Soul and Spirit of Scripture*, 86–91. See also Crouzel, *Origen*, 87–98.

45. The Latin term here is *corpus*, by which Origen (and Rufinus as translator) refers to the first sense of meaning in the biblical passage at hand.

46. Jgs 5.3.

47. Mt 11.15.

48. Note here that Origen acknowledges his hearers to be at different levels of spiritual advancement or preparedness to hear the various levels of scriptural meaning.

49. Jgs 5.3.
50. Jgs 5.2–31.
51. Cf. Nm 21.17–18.
52. Cf. Dt 32.1–43.
53. Cf. Ex 15.1–21.
54. Cf. 1 Kgs 2.1–10 (1 Sm 2.1–10).
55. 1 Chr 16.8–36.

divine songs have been recorded. Therefore, here the voice of the just one says: "I will sing to the Lord and sing psalms to the God of Israel."[56] Who, do you think, is of a voice so melodious and of a spirit so pure and a mind so sincere that his old song is able to please his [God's] divine hearing? Truly, he is that one who has in himself no harsh noise of sin, who has nothing offensive on his tongue, who carries nothing of ignorant rudeness in his spirit. He can rightly say: "I will sing to the Lord, I will sing psalms to the God of Israel."

4. But because we do not rush to explain the succession of the song verse by verse, altering at all events the sequence of the reading, let us see what it is that he says: "My heart [has been turned] to things that have been arranged for this Israel."[57] This seems to me to be what he says: My heart and my soul[58] and my understanding[59] and my whole mind[60] are directed toward and look toward that "which has been arranged" and which has been prepared "for Israel"; with my whole mind I look forward to what is about to happen. For if I direct the soul[61] to that, all things that are in this world "I will count as dung that I may gain Christ,"[62] who "has prepared for those who love him" all those things "which the eye has not seen and ear has not heard nor has risen up in the heart of man."[63] Accordingly, "my heart," it is said, "is stretched out toward those things." For I do not any longer carry the heart of a man, nor do I think what I think ac-

---

56. Jgs 5.3.
57. Jgs 5.9.
58. The term here for "soul" is *animus*, which, as well as "spirit," can mean the rational part of the soul, or "mind." Usually this translation uses "spirit" for *animus*, but here it employs "soul" because the statement suggests that all parts of the human person that can be otherwise directed are here directed toward what God has prepared for Israel, and the spirit, in Origen's tripartite anthropology, can never be directed toward anything but God and his works, since it is in the image of God's own Spirit. Again, see discussion of Origen's anthropology in Dively Lauro, *The Soul and Spirit of Scripture*, 86–91.
59. The term for "understanding" here is *sensus*.
60. The term for "mind" here is *mens*.
61. Again, the term for "soul" here is *animus*. See explanation in n. 58, above.
62. Cf. Phil 3.8.
63. Cf. 1 Cor 2.9.

cording to man; but, because according to Scripture those "to whom the word of God is directed are gods,"[64] nor do I see[65] these things according to human understanding, but by a divine understanding.[66]

5. "Powerful men of the people, bless the Lord, you who have risen above the beasts of burden."[67] What is it "to have risen above a beast of burden"? This, my body, is a "beast of burden," for it has been given in order to assist and to serve the soul.[68] But I am, that is, the interior man is, that one "who has risen above" this "beast of burden." With reference to him it is said, "I shall bless the Lord." Therefore, if truly you have risen above the body, and you have been made superior to bodily desires, and the movements of your body are directed by the bridle of the mind[69] and by the direction of the interior man, it is said about you that "you have risen above the beast of burden" so that "you may bless the Lord."

Yet what is that which follows? It is said, "Those sitting on top of carriages and those on top of brightly shining she-asses."[70] What seems to be the "brightly shining she-asses"? For Scripture says that it is necessary "for those who are sitting on top of carriages and on top of brightly shining she-asses" to "bless the Lord." For example, it seems to me, some such thing is found in especially difficult passages: when this beast of burden, that is, my body, has come under the yoke of the word of God, then "the

---

64. Cf. Jn 10.34–35. Note Origen's reference to the human's divinization at the hands of God's grace.

65. The term here for "see," *prospicio*, has the connotation of "looking ahead to" or "foreseeing."

66. The term for these two occurrences of "understanding" is *mens*, usually rendered in this translation as "mind."

67. Jgs 5.9–10.

68. The term for "soul" here is *anima*, and the term for "body" is *corpus*. In Origen's anthropology, the right order of the human parts requires that the body submit to the direction of the soul, and the soul, in turn, to the direction of the spirit, which is in the image of God's own Spirit. See nn. 44 and 58, above, on anthropology.

69. The term for "mind" here is *mens*, and Origen understands the mind to be the rational part of the human soul. See Crouzel, *Origen*, 88.

70. Cf. Jgs 5.10.

carriage" of my body[71] will begin "to shine brightly," and this "she-ass," that is, my flesh,[72] will then be said "to shine brightly" when she has adorned herself in the splendor of chastity and modesty. And so rightly it is said, the soul,[73] "sitting on top of a brightly shining she-ass blesses the Lord" and, in the middle of rejoicing, praises him.[74]

"There they will dedicate works of righteousness to the Lord."[75] That sacrifice "to the Lord" is "acceptable"[76] which is offered to God by way of righteousness and justice. And, for that reason, it is said: "The righteous have been greatly strengthened in Israel."[77] Indeed, in other nations, they who are stronger by vigor of body are called powerful in battle, but in Israel they who are more righteous are themselves called greater powers in war, because righteousness, even if it is weak in force, conquers, but unrighteousness, even if it has harbored many powerful defenders, is conquered. So, therefore, in this our nation, that is, among the people of God, either we conquer through righteousness or we are conquered through unrighteousness.

6. "Rise up, Deborah, rise up and arouse 10,000 of the people."[78] When does prophecy "rise up"? Certainly at the advent of Christ. And not only does she "raise" herself "up," but she also "arouses" the people toward believing. "You shall lead the captives from captivity, son of Abinoam."[79] "Abinoam" means "the response of the father." His son is Barak. "He" who has observed the responses of the Father of heaven "will seize captivity" from the enemies. "Lord, humble for me those who are stronger than I am."[80] That is the cry of the faithful ones confessing that their

---

71. Again, the term for the occurrences of "body" here is *corpus*.

72. The term for "flesh" here is *caro, carnis,* and for Origen it represents the base tendencies within the "body," or *corpus*. See nn. 44, 58, and 68, above, on anthropology.

73. The term here for "soul" is *anima*.

74. Cf. Ps 21.23 (22.22) and Heb 2.12.

75. Jgs 5.11 (LXX; wording not in RSV).

76. Cf. 1 Pt 2.5 and Rom 12.1.

77. Cf. Jgs 5.11 (LXX; wording not in RSV).

78. Cf. Jgs 5.12.

79. Jgs 5.12.

80. Jgs 5.13 (LXX; wording not in RSV).

enemies are simply stronger, [the enemies] against whom the battle is fought also for us, since "for us it is not a battle against flesh and blood"—otherwise the adversary would not be stronger than we are—but because "for us the wrestling is against principalities and powers and against the rulers of this world of darkness and against spirits of wickedness."[81] For that reason the prophet [Deborah][82] says: "Lord, humble for me those stronger than I am."[83] For how may this so very great power of the spirits not be far more powerful than human fragility? But in him, Christ, God "aids us in our weakness,"[84] in relation to whom the Apostle says: "I can do all things in him who strengthens me greatly,"[85] Christ. Therefore, those powers are truly stronger than we are, but, again, Christ, who is in us and strengthens us greatly, is stronger than all things, "to whom are glory and dominion forever and ever. Amen."[86]

81. Eph. 6.12.
82. Note that here Origen (or Rufinus as translator) for the first time since early in *Hom in Jgs* 5 refers to Deborah as a "prophet," *propheta,* rather than as "prophecy," *prophetia.*
83. Jgs 5.13 (LXX; wording not in RSV).
84. Cf. Rom 8.26.
85. Phil 4.13.
86. 1 Pt 4.11.

HOMILY SEVEN

*Concerning this: that the people of Israel were
handed over into the hands of Midian*[1]

"THE LAND IS AT peace,"[2] so long as sin is in repose. But it is said that the land is stirred up, that is, those who dwell in the land, when sins have begun to stir up and disturb thoroughly the souls[3] of men. And, for that reason, this is written which now the present reading contains: "And the land," it is said, "was at peace for forty years."[4] "And the people of Israel did evil in the sight of the Lord, and the Lord handed them over into the hands of Midian for seven years. And Midian prevailed over Israel."[5] Therefore, so long as righteousness was in the land, that is, in those who dwelled in the land, it is said, "the land was at peace."[6] But when injustice increased and "they did evil in the sight of the Lord," then "the Lord," it is said, "handed them over into the hands of Midian for seven years." The Midianites are not said to have prevailed over the people of the Lord as long as the people kept the commandments of the Lord. But when they began to disregard the divine commands, the hand of the enemies was made stronger and more powerful against them. And against that first people, indeed, the bodily enemies rose up in power whenever they [the first people] had committed sin, and, indeed, against us also who are called Israel according to the spirit, without doubt, the spiritual enemy grows in power when we disregard the commands of God. When we defy the commandments of Christ, the hand of the

---

1. Cf. Jgs 6.1.   2. Jgs 5.31.
3. The term here for "souls" is from *anima*.
4. Jgs 5.31.   5. Jgs 6.1–2.
6. Cf. Ezek 4.1–3.

demons is made stronger against us, and we also are handed over to enemies when we sever ourselves from grace.

2. But let us see what happens to those who are handed over on account of their sins. "And the people of Israel," it is said, "out of the sight of Midian made dwellings in the mountains and in caves and in fortifications, and it happened, whenever the man of Israel had planted, Midian and Amalek and the people of the East rose up over them and overcame them and destroyed all the fruits of the land as far as the border of Gaza."[7] He who was "according to the flesh of Israel"[8] indeed suffered these things. He sowed the land, but, on account of his sins, he had been handed over to the enemies who were growing in power. Instead of the fruits of the earth, "he reaped corruption."[9] But for us who are given the name of Israel according to the spirit, let us consider what sort of thing can happen. There is a circumstance when we sow, and the enemies cannot destroy the seeds that we sow, and they cannot plot against our cultivation of the land, but there is a circumstance when we plant, and the things we plant are destroyed.

Let Paul, the Apostle, teach us about this difference of sowing. Therefore, hear what he says: "He who sows," it is said, "in the flesh will reap corruption according to the flesh, and he who sows in the spirit will reap eternal life according to the spirit."[10] Therefore, those whose seeds the Midianites destroy are those "who sow in the flesh." They are those whose "fruits are destroyed" and perish. But those seeds that "are sown in the spirit" the Midianites cannot destroy. For adverse powers cannot rise up to spiritual fields and desecrate the fallow fields of the spirit of those who "do not sow upon the thorns, but renew fallow fields for themselves."[11]

Moreover, this is to be added, for I want to impress upon you,

---

7. Jgs 6.2–4.
8. Cf. 1 Cor 10.18 (Vulgata; RSV text differs).
9. Cf. Gal 6.8.
10. Gal 6.8. The term for "spirit" is *spiritus*.
11. Cf. Jer 4.3; Hos 10.12; Mt 13.22. The term for "fallow fields" here, *novalia*, from the adjective *novalis-e*, can also be translated as "unploughed" or "ploughed anew" or "cultivated."

and myself as well,[12] concerning the security of seeds and the care of "spiritual fruits":[13] It happens frequently that someone, exerting himself much in spiritual labor, has produced many fruits and has filled up his storehouses with the fruits of justice and has laid up many good works in the chamber of his conscience, but, if afterwards he should become negligent and after his labor he should turn more readily to pleasures and excesses, all those seeds of good works and fruits of holy work will be destroyed by dominating lust. For when sin has entered into and taken captive the human mind[14] so that it no longer has regard for the commands of God nor willingly ascends the arduous road of virtue, all things perish utterly which had been gathered together previously in the storehouses of his conscience. Therefore, the warning of the holy Scripture to be heeded by us is from the passage saying, "With all vigilance, guard your heart."[15]

Therefore, it is necessary "to guard the heart" from every sin, and especially in the time of persecution. For if it happens to someone that at some time, for example, he gathers together the fruits of justice and seeks out virtuous works and adorns himself with all the most laudable disciplines, but in the time of persecution he rejects the faith, that one has emptied out all his reserves and has become suddenly naked and empty of all his riches, because all the [fruits of] labor that were procured over a long period of time and brought together with difficulty by much sweat were suddenly squandered. And, as the prophet says, "All his deeds of justice which he did will not be remembered."[16] Therefore, Brothers, let us beseech the Lord, confessing our weakness to him, lest "he hand" us "over into the hands of Midian," "lest he hand over to the beasts the soul which makes confession to him,"[17] lest he hand us over into the power of those

---

12. Note that Origen instructs himself here openly as well, admitting his own need, and not just his audience's need, for continued spiritual growth.
13. Cf. Gal 5.22.
14. The term for "mind" here is *sensum,* which has both cognitive and affective implications.
15. Prv 4.23.   16. Cf. Ezek 3.20.
17. Cf. Ps 73.19 (74.19).

HOMILY SEVEN

who say, When will the time come when power against Christians may be given to us, when those who themselves say that they possess or know[18] God will be handed over into our hands? And what if we should be handed over and they were to take away our power? Then let us pray to receive virtue from God so that we may be able to keep firm, so that our faith in times of oppressions and tribulations may become more clear, so that by our patience their shamelessness may be overcome, and, as the Lord said, "by our endurance let us secure our souls,"[19] because "tribulation produces endurance, indeed endurance produces assent to belief, and assent to belief produces hope."[20]

For our "assent to belief" extends not only all the way to whippings, but it reaches all the way to the shedding[21] of blood, because even Christ, whom we follow, has shed his blood for our redemption,[22] so that thereafter we may go forth washed in our blood. For the baptism of blood alone[23] is what may render us more clean than the baptism of water has rendered us. And I do not presume[24] this, but Scripture reports [it], with the Lord saying to the disciples: "I have a baptism to be baptized with about which you do not know.[25] And how I am pressed that it should be accomplished!"[26] For you see that he spoke about "baptism" as the shedding of his blood. And if I do not shock by saying these things, I suspect that this baptism is higher than that other baptism which is delivered by means of water. For with that baptism [of water][27] received, certainly there are few so blessed

---

18. The term for "know" here is *nosse,* which is an infinitive form of *nosco,* and means "to have knowledge of" or "become acquainted with."

19. Cf. Lk 21.19.

20. Rom 5.3–4.

21. The Latin term here for "shedding," *profusio,* from *profundo,* also means "pouring out" or "profusion."

22. Rv 5.9.

23. Cf.. *Exhortation to Martyrdom* 30.

24. The Latin term *praesumo* also means "assume."

25. The term for "not know" here is *nescitis* from *nescio.*

26. Lk 12.50.

27. The term *illud* means "that," and Origen/Rufinus here uses it to refer to the baptism of water, while he uses *hoc,* or "this," or *istud,* meaning "that," in a more emphatic way than *illud,* to refer to the baptism of blood, or martyrdom. Also, below Rufinus uses *ibi,* meaning "there," to refer to the baptism of

who could remain immaculate continuously to the end of life, but he who has been baptized with this baptism [of blood] cannot sin any longer. And if it is not rash to venture an opinion in such things, we can say that past sins are purged by that baptism [of water], but by that other one [of blood] future sins are also thwarted. There [with water] sins are cast down; here [with blood] sins are prevented.

If God were to grant that I be washed in my own blood, that I might obtain the second baptism [of blood] by a death accepted for the sake of Christ, I, fearless, would depart from that age, so that, coming to my soul as it departs from this life, "the ruler of this world"[28] would not find anyone, but rather he also would be laid to rest[29] by the shedding of my blood and would not dare to accuse anyone's soul that is soaked by his own blood, glorified by his own death, washed in his own blood. After that baptism [of blood], the Midianites no longer would rush in[30] in order to ruin and destroy the fruits of the soul. For who could follow the soul of the martyr, which, elevated above all "the powers on high,"[31] inclines itself[32] toward the heavenly altar? For the souls of the martyrs placed there "under the altar"[33] of God are said to cry out during the days and the nights, saying: "Lord, you who are just and true, how long before you avenge our blood upon those who dwell on earth?"[34] For placed there, [the souls of martyrs] take their stand at the divine sacrifices.

Indeed, they are blessed who merit these things. They are blessed whose heart, when they retreat from this age, does not tremble before sin, whom, going on to the Lord, the dread of sins does not scare away. Blessed is that soul which, by the pro-

---

water, and *hic*, meaning "here," to refer to the baptism of blood. In all these cases, the translation uses brackets in the text to make it read more clearly.

28. Cf. Jn 12.31.
29. The term for "laid to rest" here is *sopiretur*, which can also be translated as "killed" in the passive.
30. The term for "rush in," *irruo* or *inruo*, can imply an attack or invasion.
31. Cf. Eph 2.2. The term for "on high," *aerias*, can also mean "of the air."
32. The term for "inclines," from *tendo*, can also be translated as "extends" or "directs."
33. Rv 6.9.
34. Rv 6.10.

fuse shedding of blood in martyrdom, beats down the aerial troops of demons who are attacking it. Blessed is the one about whom, as he goes to heaven, the angels say that prophetic word: "Who is that one who comes up out of Bozrah?"[35] that is, he who ascends out of the flesh up to heaven, "who is he who comes up out of Bozrah, the redness in his vestments?"[36]—indicating in "the redness of vestments" the shedding of blood. Accordingly, blessed are the souls who follow Christ along the same path on which Christ preceded them. And for that reason, because they follow in this way, they come all the way to the altar of God itself where resides the Lord Jesus Christ himself, "high priest of the good things to come,"[37] "to whom are glory and power forever and ever. Amen."[38]

35. Cf. Is 63.1–2. 36. Cf. ibid.
37. Cf. Heb 9.11.
38. Cf. 1 Pt 4.11. In all the homilies except for this one (*Homily* 7), the word *imperium* occurs in the final sentence and is translated as "dominion." In this homily alone, however, instead of *gloria et imperium,* the words *gloria et potestas* occur, and *potestas* is translated here as "power." Perhaps Origen (and Rufinus as translator), after discussing physical martyrdom, intended to stress the power of Christ's own baptism of blood for the salvation of all.

HOMILY EIGHT

On the people of the East and on Gideon in part

MEN,[1] THE Midianites, whose name means "outside judgment," came together against Israel. Amen, they came together against Israel, they who are outside the judgment of God and "who have sinned outside of the law, and outside the law will perish."[2] Amen, Amalek also came together, whose name itself means "the people who squander."[3] Amen, this earthly race also came to attack, devoted both to stomach and to appetite. It was carnal Israel coming together to attack spiritual Israel. What does this mean, that the "people of the East"[4] also are joined to them and are said to come with them in order to attack Israel?[5]

For the hearer says to me: if it were written that "the people" of the West "came together with them," I would ask nothing, for you would say to me, by means of the laws of allegory, that the people of the West are people of darkness and they join themselves to those nations which either are outside the judgment of God or, devoted to the stomach, attack those who strive to see

---

1. The term here for "amen" throughout this homily is *esto*, which is the future imperative, second or third person singular of the verb *sum*, "to be." It can be translated "so be it," "let it be," "so shall it be," or "amen."

2. Rom 2.12.

3. The term for "squander" here is *ablingens*, from *ablingo*, which literally means "to lick away."

4. Note that the East, where the sun rises, is a biblical figure for salvation and the Messiah, who is called "Sun of Justice" in Mal 3.20 (4.2). See Eph 5.8 for the idea that Christians are the people of the light. Here though, Origen is referring to those who call themselves Christians but indeed are heretics who divide the Church and distort the faith.

5. Cf. Jgs 6.3.

HOMILY EIGHT 101

God with the mind.[6] Yet, now, when it is said that "the people of the East came with Midian and Amalek,"[7] how can these things be explained properly? Therefore, let us see if we can find in such difficult passages in Scripture some worthy meaning in these divine pages.

Everyone who takes upon himself in any way the name of Christ becomes "a person of the East."[8] For so it is written of Christ: "Behold the man, his name is 'the East.'"[9] Accordingly, everyone who takes on the name of Christ is said to be "a person of the East," but not always does he who takes on the name of Christ also remain in the Church of Christ. Therefore, if you see that the heretics have spoken of themselves by using the name of Christ but take by storm the Church of Christ and bring together troops against the faith of Christ and attack the people of the Lord and stir up wars against the universal[10] faith, I do not want you to hesitate to say about them that they are truly "people of the East." With the Midianites and with Amalek they come to take by storm the people of God, because, togeth-

---

6. The term for "mind" here is *mens*.
7. Cf. Jgs 6.3.
8. The Latin word *filius* can mean "son" or "people," and this translation employs "people" in these homilies wherever Origen (or translator Rufinus) refers to Israel or to a foreign nation.
9. Zec 6.12 (LXX; RSV="Branch"). Note that *Oriens* for "the East" is in the Vulgate and renders into Latin the term in the LXX, *anatole*, which refers to a rising or sunrise or the east, and can also be translated as "Rising Sun" or "Morning," which, on the one hand, is a reference to the Messiah—see Hg 2.20–23—but, on the other hand, is a possible name for Satan or Lucifer himself, who was known as the "Angel of the Dawn" or "Rising Sun" before his fall from grace. (A tradition of viewing Satan as the Angel of the Morning Star or Dawn, who falls from heaven because of his prideful belief that he can set himself above God, stems from Is 14.12–22, wherein the king of Babylon becomes a figure of Satan. A similar account is found in Ezek 28.11–19, wherein the Prince of Tyre becomes a figure of Satan. For commentary, see Crouzel, *Origen*, 212–13. Enoch also refers to Satan as the one among God's angels burning bright with flames who fell from heaven out of pride. See the account of creation at 2 Enoch 29.3–5 and the account of the temptation and fall of Adam at 2 Enoch 31.4.) Again, here, Origen is referring to heretics who, implicitly under the grip of Satan, divide the Church and distort the faith.
10. The term for "universal" here is *catholicus*, which can be translated as "orthodox" or "universal."

er with the pagans and the Jews, the heretics also persecute the Church of God. And, I believe, they are the ones who are signified by "the people of the East."[11]

2. It is said, "Therefore, all of Midian and Amalek and the people of the East came together and rose up and overcame them and pitched camp in the valley of Jezreel."[12] Those who want to attack the people of God "set up camp in the valleys," in sunken[13] and low-lying[14] places—"in the valley," it is said, "of Jezreel." Now, we find that "Jezreel" means "the seed of God." Do you see where the enemies "set up camp"? They did not dare to go to that place where "the fruits of the Spirit"[15] seem already to have been born, but to the place where the seed of God still lies dormant, where the fruit has not yet risen up. For he who "has gone out to sow sows the word"[16] over every place, but hear the Lord himself saying that the seed of God is used to suffering: "Some have fallen along the path, and the birds of the sky, coming by, tear them away."[17] See what he himself [Jesus] says, interpreting in the following verses: "But they who were sown along the path, they are those who hear the word of God and receive it with joy, but the Devil[18] comes and takes away from their heart that which has been sown."[19] So, therefore, even those now come to the seed of God and wish to "take" it "away from the heart" of those in whom it was sown, because they find them settled in the valleys, already pursuing each one of the lowest places. For from these places come those who, basely and un-

---

11. See *Hom in Nm* 25.1 on the double meaning of "East"—for the Son of God, on the one hand, and for Lucifer, on the other. See also n. 9, above.

12. Jgs 6.33.

13. The term for "sunken" here, *dejectus,* can also refer to an emotional state of despair or dejection.

14. The term for "low-lying" here, *humilis,* can also imply lowly status or insignificance.

15. Cf. Gal 5.22.   16. Cf. Mk 4.3–14.

17. Mk 4.4 and cf. Mk 4.15.

18. The term for "the Devil" here is *Zabulus,* which is the collateral form of the Greek word *Diabolos.* The Latin translation of these homilies sometimes employs *Zabulus* and sometimes *Satanus,* and, though this English translation views them as synonymous, it tends to translate *Zabulus* as "the Devil" and *Satanus* as "Satan."

19. Mk 4.15 and Lk 8.12.

HOMILY EIGHT 103

worthily, as so I might say, receive the word of God with a Jewish understanding,[20] and, for that reason, the demons can "tear" it "out of their heart." But he who ascends[21] from the lowness of the letter to the heights of the spirit, and, shrinking back from the fleshly meaning,[22] pursues into the higher places "those [gifts] which are of the Spirit of God,"[23] from him neither the Midianites nor the Amalekites can tear away anything, but indeed neither will "the people of the East" themselves be able to plunder the one who is established at the highest summit of spiritual understanding.[24]

3. Then, they "set up camp in the valleys."[25] "But the spirit," it is said, "of God greatly strengthened Gideon and he sounded the signal for war on the horn-shaped war-trumpet and called out for the Abiezrites to follow after him."[26] Indeed, the coherence of the exegesis required another order of explanation, but because we now speak not so much commenting on the Scriptures as consoling the people about these things that have been read aloud, we treat all those particular things which present themselves here and there. It is said, "he called out for Abiezer to follow after him," who at any rate did not exist.[27] Now, "Abiezer" means "the aid of my father." Accordingly, Gideon seems to have called upon not any man but upon "the aid of" the sovereign

---

20. The term for "understanding" here is *intellectus*.
21. The term for "ascend" here is *conscendo*, which, like *ascendo*, means "to ascend" but also means "to mount" or "embark on a ship," while *ascendo* also means "to mount up," "rise up," "go up," or "grow up."
22. The term for "meaning" here is *intelligentia* and refers here to the first (that is, bodily or historical) meaning of Scripture. See *De principiis* 4 and Dively Lauro, *The Soul and Spirit of Scripture*.
23. 1 Cor 2.14.
24. The term for "understanding" here is *intelligentia* and refers here to the third (that is, spiritual or pneumatic) meaning of Scripture, that is, the higher of the two non-literal senses of scriptural meanings. Again, see *De principiis* 4 and Dively Lauro, *The Soul and Spirit of Scripture*.
25. Cf. Jgs 6.33. The term for "camp" here, *castra*, has the connotation of "military camp."
26. Jgs 6.34.
27. Abiezer is a male descendant of Manasseh, who was a son of Joseph, and so is a family of the tribe of Manasseh (Jos 17.2). Gideon is an Abiezrite (Jgs 6.11). Here, Origen refers to Abiezer as a family name, not an individual.

"Father." Meanwhile, he also sends for the auxiliary troops to assemble. The people assemble and the whole army is gathered together near Gideon.[28]

4. It is said, "And then Gideon said to God: 'If you save Israel by my hand, just as you have said, here I am and I will place a fleece of wool on the threshing floor, and, if indeed dew should fall on top of the fleece and dryness should occur over all the ground, then I will know that you will save Israel by my hand, as you have said.' And it was so."[29] When there are so many innumerable signs or prophetic portents that Gideon could ask from God in order to confirm God's promise, why did it seem right to him, after the angelic voice and heavenly promise,[30] to ask for such an unusual sign from God? For he says: "I will place a fleece of wool on the threshing floor, and if dew should be on top of the fleece alone and there should be dryness over all the ground, then I will be confident that you will save Israel by my hand."[31] And when Gideon had earnestly requested that sign from God, it happened.

But amen, O Gideon, you have obtained the efficacy of a sign, so why do you also take "a fleece of wool" and "wring it out into a basin"?[32] What influenced you to do this? But, amen, you have obtained the first sign, then why is it that you still should ask for a second sign in a reversed and completely changed order?[33] For perhaps someone from among those who listen more attentively to what is read says that these things do not seem to be consistent with what is written, which the law decreed: "You shall not test the Lord your God."[34] But the result of the matter shows that he did not act contrary to the command, for God would not have given heed to a petition that demands something against the law.

But now especially let us see that in the first sign "the dew" indeed "fell over the fleece of wool, yet dryness resulted on the whole ground,"[35] and in the second sign "the dew fell over the

---

28. Cf. Jgs 6.35.
29. Jgs 6.36–38.
30. Cf. Jgs 6.14–16.
31. Jgs 6.37.
32. Cf. Jgs 6.38.
33. Cf. Jgs 6.39–40.
34. Dt 6.16.
35. Cf. Jgs 6.37–38.

whole ground, while there was dryness on the fleece,"[36] and in this way Gideon received assurance that the Lord would save Israel by his [Gideon's] hand. The reason for this mystery must be seen, concerning which I remember that a certain one of our predecessors said in his writings that "the fleece of wool" is the people of Israel, yet they represented the remaining ground as the rest of the nations, and the "dew" which fell "over the fleece" is the word of God, which had been conferred on this people alone from heaven. For only upon Israel had the "dew" of divine legislation come, but dryness possessed all the nations because no moisture of the Divine Word was poured over them.[37]

But the reason that the second sign changed completely into the reverse, for which it says: "Considering that dew comes down over the whole ground, while dryness remains upon the fleece,"[38] is understood as follows. See all this people, who were gathered together from the nations throughout the whole earth, now possessing within themselves the divine dew; see them poured over with the dew of Moses, moistened with the writings of the prophets; see them also growing verdant with the evangelical and apostolic moisture, while that fleece, that is, the Jewish people, are suffering a dryness and aridity for the word of God, according to what is written, that: "The people of Israel will be for a long time without a king, without a leader, without a prophet; there will be neither altar, nor host, nor sacrifice."[39] You consider how much "dryness" remains with them, how much aridity of the Divine Word befalls them. Indeed, these things, as it

36. Cf. Jgs 6.39–40.
37. As mentioned in the Introduction to this translation in the present volume, the predecessors to whom Origen refers here are unknown. It is arguable, however, that Origen is referring to a Jewish tradition of interpreting the elements of Gideon's test with these types. Such is the suggestion of G. Bardy in "Les traditions juives dans l'œuvre d'Origène," *Revue biblique* 34 (1925): 217–52. The same Christian interpretation (more specifically, the same pneumatic or spiritual reading) of Gideon's two requests, with the fleece as juxtaposing the Jews and the Church, is found after Origen in Theodoret (c. 393–c. 466), Bishop of Cyrrhus, in *Quaestiones in Iudices* 6.15 (PG 80:501). See *Origène: Homélies sur Les Juges,* SC 389, 194, n. 1.
38. Cf. Jgs 6.39–40.
39. Cf. Hos 3.4.

is fitting to acknowledge, were gathered together for us by the work[40] of the ancestors; but because even we, by the word heard from the sages, as it is written,[41] must commend and add to that, let us see what we also may be able to build upon concerning such things.

For indeed, when often I would be meditating by myself on the 71st Psalm,[42] it struck me that, when in it it represented[43] the coming of Christ, in this very passage it declares what is going to happen: It is said, "And he[44] will come down like rain on the fleece and like raindrops trickling[45] onto the ground."[46] Here "fleece" is mentioned, and in the Psalms "fleece" is written. Namely, "he[47] will come down like rain," it is said, "upon the fleece." Therefore, he "comes down on" that "fleece," that is, the people of the circumcision, and "as raindrops trickling onto the ground," that is, upon the rest of the ground, our Lord Jesus Christ comes down "dripping" also "onto" us and imparting also to us, the gentiles,[48] drops of heavenly dew, so that we, who, dried by a continuous drought, were "upon" all "the earth," also may drink. So then, holy Gideon,[49] reflecting with a prophetic spirit upon this order of mystery, not only requested from God the first sign, but also demands a second sign in reverse order. For he knew the divine "dew," which is the advent of the Son of God, which is to come not only to the Jews, but also afterwards to the gentiles, since indeed from the "disbelief" of Israel "salvation

---

40. The term for "work," here *labor*, can also be translated as "hardship" or "suffering."

41. Cf. Prv 9.9.

42. It is the 72d Psalm in RSV. Jews and Christians view this psalm as anticipating the Messiah. See also Is 9.2–7 and 11.1–9.

43. Origen means that it foreshadowed or referred allegorically to the coming of Christ.

44. Origen refers allegorically to Christ here.

45. The term here for "trickling," *stillantia*, from *stillo*, can also be translated as "dripping," meaning "coming down slowly."

46. Ps 71.6 (72.6).

47. Again, this refers allegorically to Christ.

48. The term for "gentiles" here, *gentibus*, also means "nations" or "foreigners."

49. See Heb 11.32–34 for the New Testament designation of Gideon as "holy."

comes to the gentiles."[50] And this is why, on account of the dryness of the fleece, the whole earth is poured over with the grace of divine dew.

Moreover, in this deed of Gideon, a very faithful man, that thing must not be passed over in the least, I believe, which for us can resemble a kind of spiritual caution. "He saw an angel,"[51] but the learned man, having also already the example of the predecessor Jesus [son of Nun],[52] acts more cautiously. For he knew that it is possible that even the angels of darkness "transfigure[53] themselves into angels of light,"[54] and, for that reason, with the most cautious examination, it is said, I want "to test the spirit, whether it is from God,"[55] because "the spiritual man examines all things."[56] For his predecessor Jesus son of Nun had done so, who, when he had seen "the leader of the heavenly host," inquired into and investigated whether "he is of us or of our enemies."[57] In this way even the most holy Gideon investigates the angelic vision by a variety and reversal of signs.

5. Moreover, how does what Gideon says seem to you: "I will place the fleece"—not just anywhere, not in the field or in the forest, but "on the threshing floor"?[58] He says, "On the threshing floor," where the "harvest" is, "for the harvest is abundant, but the laborers are few."[59] "I will place," it is said, "the fleece" there where "the harvest" is. What had provoked the holy man Gideon, or what vision had possessed him to do this? For he foresaw by the Spirit that Christ "gathers together" his people on "the threshing floor," and there he cleanses[60] them "while holding in his hand a winnowing-fork," and there he separates "the chaff" from the grain.[61] Therefore, not without reason a

---

50. Cf. Rom 11.30–31. 51. Cf. Jgs 6.12.
52. Cf. Jos 5.13.
53. The term *transfigurare*, when joined with *se*, as here, means "to pretend to be," or "to take on a false appearance."
54. Cf. 2 Cor 11.14. 55. 1 Jn 4.1.
56. 1 Cor 2.15 and cf. *Hom in Nm* 27.11–12.
57. Cf. Jos 5.13–14. 58. Jgs 6.37.
59. Mt 9.37.
60. The term for "cleanses" here, *expugno*, also means "to justify" or "vindicate" of sins.
61. Cf. Mt 3.12.

man so great and of such [good] character, of whom even the holy Apostle when writing to the Hebrews makes mention in the enumeration of names[62] of the prophets, selected "the threshing floor" for placing down the fleece. And not without reason "did he squeeze out the fleece into the basin and fill it up with water."[63]

Also, concerning this matter, let us search in the holy Scriptures [to see] whether there is presented to us some opportunity for understanding even this. Let us come to the Gospel. We find there that our Lord and Savior, "stripping himself of his garments and having girded himself with a linen cloth, puts water into a basin and washes his disciples' feet."[64] Therefore, you see that these sayings of the prophet represented in shadows those things which had to be fulfilled in the last times by the Lord. Accordingly, that "water" which "Jesus put into the basin" was the dew of heavenly grace, from which "he washed the feet of his disciples." And for that reason he justly said to them: "You are now clean because of the word which I have spoken to you."[65] Moreover, we, if only we would present our feet, the Lord Jesus is ready "to wash the feet" of our soul and cleanse them with heavenly dew, with the grace of the Holy Spirit, with the word of knowledge.[66] For he did not want the apostles alone to be "clean," but also all who believe on account of his word.[67] And to all believers he says what he said to Peter: "Unless I shall have washed you, you will have no part with me."[68] For it is certain that no one may have a part with Christ, unless he has been washed and made clean.[69]

Come, I pray, Lord Jesus, Son of God, "strip yourself of garments," which because of me you wore, and be girded on account of me, and "put water into a basin and wash the feet" of your servants, wash away the filth from your sons and daughters. "Wash the feet" of our soul, so that, imitating you and following you, "we may strip ourselves" of the old "garments" and may say: "At night I stripped myself of my garment; how will I put it

---

62. Cf. Heb 11.32.
63. Cf. Jgs 6.38.
64. Cf. Jn 13.4–5.
65. Jn 15.3.
66. See n. 79, below.
67. Cf. Jn 17.20.
68. Jn 13.8.
69. See *Comm in Jn* 32.4–18.

back on?"⁷⁰ and again that we may say: "I have washed my feet; how will I make them dirty again?"⁷¹ For as soon as "you have washed" my "feet," also you give me a chance to lie down with you so that I may hear from you: "You call me Lord and Teacher, and you speak rightly, for I am. If then I, Lord and Teacher, have washed your feet, then wash also one another's feet."⁷²

Therefore, I also wish now "to wash the feet" of my brothers,⁷³ "to wash the feet" of my co-disciples.⁷⁴ And for that reason I take the water⁷⁵ that I draw from the fountains of Israel,⁷⁶ yes indeed, which "I press out" of the Israelitic "fleece." For I now press out the water from the "fleece" of the book of Judges, and at another time water from the "fleece" of the book of Kings, and water from the "fleece" of Isaiah or Jeremiah, and "I put" it "into the basin" of my soul, taking the meaning⁷⁷ into my heart. And I receive the feet of those who present themselves and prepare themselves for washing, and, to whatever extent I am able,⁷⁸ I wish "to wash the feet" of my brothers and to fulfill the command of the Lord, so that by the word of true knowledge⁷⁹ the listeners may be cleansed from the filth of sins,⁸⁰ so that they may cast off from themselves every impurity⁸¹ of the vices and

70. Song 5.3.
71. Ibid.
72. Jn 13.13–14. Note that Origen here calls for the preacher to wash the souls of his audience with the sacramental—grace-filled—water of the Scriptures.
73. Note that Origen here is responding affirmatively to Jesus' call for the preacher to wash the souls of his hearers with the sacramental—grace-filled—water of the Scriptures.
74. The term here for "co-disciple," *condiscipulus,* means "schoolmate" or "companion." By this term Origen is here putting himself on equal footing with his audience members, the congregation, that is, all other believers.
75. Cf. Is 12.3.
76. Cf. Ps 67.27 (68.26).
77. The term here for "meaning" is *sensus.*
78. The term here for "I am able" is *praevaleo,* which can mean "I have the power" or "I prevail" or "I am more able."
79. The term here for "knowledge" is *doctrina,* which can also be translated as "teaching."
80. Cf. Ezek 24.13.
81. The term here for "impurity," *immunditia,* can also be translated as "uncleanness" or "filth."

possess clean "feet" which rightly may advance[82] "toward the preparation of the Gospel of peace,"[83] so that all of us, purified together in Christ through the word, may not be cast away from the marriage chamber of the Bridegroom on account of dirty clothes,[84] but with dazzling white garments, washed feet, a "clean heart,"[85] may recline at the wedding banquet of the Bridegroom, of our Lord Jesus Christ himself, "to whom are glory and dominion forever and ever. Amen."[86]

82. The term for "advance," *ingredior,* can imply the commencement or inception of an action.
83. Cf. Eph 6.15.
84. Cf. Mt 22.11–13 and Zec 3.3–5.
85. Cf. Mt 5.8.
86. 1 Pt 4.11.

HOMILY NINE

Again, the rest on Gideon, and on the battle that Gideon waged with 300 chosen men

RODIGIOUS was the multitude that had been gathered together against Israel so that the multitude could be compared with "locusts."[1] It is said, "And their camels were innumerable as the sand which is at the edge of the sea."[2] Therefore, let us see how this multitude of enemies, so innumerable, could have been overcome. It is said, 32,000 of the armed soldiers from the people of Israel[3] went out with Gideon ready to fight against that whole multitude. And God gave promises to Gideon, saying: "A great multitude is with you."[4] And what if "the multitude is great"? In wars, does not a more numerous army furnish more secure protections? Not at all, it is said, are divine battles executed in the same way as human battles. The glorious work of divine power is not completed if it is supported by human aids, because "a king is not saved by the great number of his power."[5] Therefore, lest by chance Israel should boast and, by boasting, should claim[6] a part of the victory, for that reason, the Lord says to Gideon: "The people with you are many. I will not hand over Midian into their hands lest by chance Israel should boast against me, saying, 'My hand saved me.' Therefore, speak into the ears of the people, saying, 'He who is fearful and full of dread at heart is to turn back.'

1. Jgs 6.5 and 7.12; cf. Ex 10.1–20, Jer 26.23 (46.23), Jl 1.4, and Am 7.1.
2. Jgs 7.12.
3. Cf. Jgs 7.3.
4. Jgs 7.2.
5. Ps 32.16 (33.16).
6. The term for "claim" here is *praesumo*, which means "to presume" or "to take to one's self" or "to take first or beforehand."

And out of the people 22,000 men turned back from Mount Gilead and 10,000 remained."⁷

Therefore, let us see first what it is that he says: "fearful and full of dread at heart."⁸ For there are two certain words by which human weakness is proven, that is, "those fearful and full of dread at heart." He can seem "afraid," even he who, at first sight, is anxious to join the fight; yet he is not terrified with his whole heart, but he can be revived and given life again. But "full of dread" is he who already, even before he sees evil things, is terrified by a single thought, just as by an in-growing vice, experiencing an icy dread throughout the limbs, so that not so much by sight as by the very hearing and expectation of evil things is he broken down. And, for that reason, he added, "full of dread at heart," for now this vice remains fixed in the "heart" and in the interior parts of the mind.⁹

What then? We say that only just then Gideon said to the people: "If anyone is fearful and full of dread at heart." Should he depart from the battles and leave the army, should he wholly desert the engagements of courageous men? Or even today the leader of our army, our Lord and Savior Jesus Christ, calls out to his soldiers and says: "If anyone is fearful and full of dread at heart."¹⁰ Should he not come to my army? For this is what indeed by other words, yet with the same meaning,¹¹ in the Gospels he says: "He who does not take up his cross and follow me is not worthy of me,"¹² and, "He who does not hate his father and mother and brothers and sisters, and indeed in addition even his own life,¹³ is not worthy of me,"¹⁴ and again, "He who

---

7. Jgs 7.2–3 and cf. Dt 20.1–4.
8. Jgs 7.3.
9. The term for "mind" here is *animus*. Since Origen understands mind to be a faculty in the soul, one could translate this term as "soul" here, but this translation strives to distinguish between Origen's uses of *anima* for "soul" and *animus* for "mind" or "spirit."
10. Jgs 7.3.
11. The term for "meaning" here is *sensus*.
12. Mt 10.38, and cf. Lk 14.27, 9.23, and Mk 8.34.
13. The term here for "life" is *anima*, which this translation usually represents as "soul," but here it uses "life" for the sake of more clarity in the English.
14. Lk 14.26.

has not renounced all the things that he possesses cannot be my disciple."[15] Does not Christ, clearly by these words, separate out "the persons who are fearful and full of dread" and sever them from his military camp? So all of you who wish to follow the army of Christ, who long to be in his military camp, banish fear far from your mind[16] and dread far from your heart, so that with confidence the soldier of Christ[17] may say, "If the military camp should make a stand against me, my heart will not be afraid; if a battle should rise up against me, in him will I hope,"[18] and he may confidently say, "The Lord is my illumination[19] and my salvation; whom shall I fear? The Lord is the protector of my life;[20] of whom shall I be afraid?"[21]

But lest that army so great should frighten you away, it contains in itself nothing difficult, nothing arduous or impossible. Do you want to know how easy it would be to fill it up with soldiers from the faith? It is often usual in those camps for even women to conquer, because it [the battle] is fought not by the strength of the body but by the power of faith. In the above, we read in this very book of Judges about the triumphs of the woman Deborah, for whom a fear caused by lack of faith did not disturb her feminine mind.[22] But what should I recount about Judith, that admirable and most noble of all women? She who, when already things were nearly lost, was not afraid to hasten alone to help and alone to subject herself and her head to death at the hand of the most savage Holofernes,[23] and proceeded to war not relying on military equipment or on war horses or on military supports[24] but on the power of the mind[25] and the con-

15. Lk 14.33.
16. The term for "mind" here is *mens*.
17. Cf. 2 Tm 2.3.   18. Ps 26.3 (27.3).
19. The term here for "illumination," *illuminatio,* can also be translated as "lighting up" or "enlightening."
20. The term here for "life" is *vita*.
21. Ps 26.1 (27.1).
22. Cf. Jgs 4.4. The term for "mind" here is *mens,* and for Origen the mind is the rational part of the soul.
23. Cf. Jdt 13.1–10.   24. Cf. Jdt 9.7.
25. The term here for "mind" is *animus,* which is often translated as "spirit" but can also mean the "mind" as the rational part of the soul.

fidence of faith. At the same time with determination and courage she killed the enemy, and the woman restored to the country the freedom that the men had lost. And why do we turn back with you to examples of ancient people so long ago? Under our eyes we often have seen the fact that women and virgins, even of a very young age, have endured to the end tyrannous torments by virtue of martyrdom, for whom to the weakness of gender were added the frailties of young life besides.

So, therefore, in those who serve as soldiers for the truth, but indeed also in those who serve as soldiers for God, fortitude, not of the body, but of the mind[26] is required, because victory is obtained not by javelins of iron but by the weapons[27] of prayers, and it is faith that supplies endurance in the fight. For this reason also the holy Apostle equips the soldiers of God with weapons appropriate to wars of this kind, by saying: "Therefore, stand clothed with the breastplate of righteousness and having girded your loins in truth; moreover, receive the helmet of salvation and the sword of the Spirit; indeed, in all things take up the shield of faith upon which you can extinguish the fiery darts of the evil one."[28] And also he orders "the feet to be shod in preparation for the Gospel of peace,"[29] and, by being armed in this way, "to take up" the standards[30] "of the cross of Christ and to follow him."[31]

This, moreover, is permitted in the army of Christ that, if ever perhaps you should feel yourself to be inferior to forces during persecutions and you should see that a struggle is not equal to you against the cruelty of tyranny because of the weak-

---

26. Again, the term here for "mind" is *animus*, in order to stress Origen's idea that what is required is not strength of the body, but strength of the mind, or rational part of the soul, in order for the soul to will to follow rightly the spirit, or image of God's own Spirit, in all things. For discussion of Origen's anthropological views, see Dively Lauro, *The Soul and Spirit of Scripture*, 86–91, and Crouzel, *Origen*, 87–98. See also *Hom in Jgs* 6.3, n. 44.

27. The term here for "weapons," from *telum*, can also be translated as "darts" or "spears."

28. Eph 6.14, 17, 16.

29. Eph 6.15.

30. The term here for "standards," from *vexillum*, can also be translated as "banners."

31. Mt 16.24; Mk 8.34; cf. Lk 14.27.

ness of the body, in this case, if you "give place to anger"[32] and flee from place to place, a military offense is not imputed to you. For also this is described in the laws of Christ, who says: "If they should persecute you in this town, flee into another; but if in the other, flee yet into another."[33] For the point of the thing is not to deny Jesus, whom you once confessed. For it is certain that he should confess him [Christ], he who for that reason flees lest he should deny him [Christ]. Therefore, if someone is "fearful" and "full of dread at heart," he should depart from the military camp, he should return to his home,[34] lest he furnish an example of fear and dread to the rest. Moreover, do you wish to see how great a crime "fear and dread" is? In the Apocalypse where those are enumerated who are to be put "into the swamp of fire," there in front of everyone he places "the persons fearful and full of dread" with those whom he counts as "unfaithful persons and fornicators and enchanters."[35] In this way, the crime of fear and dread is placed among the vast and abominable crimes. Now, we have said these things on account of those who are dismissed first from the military camp as "persons fearful and full of dread at heart."

2. But after those "22,000 departed,"[36] the Divine Word also adds, "and he says to Gideon: 'Still,'" it is said, "'the people are many. So place them down at the water and there I will test them for you.'"[37] As I see it, those who were first rejected had not gone down "to the water," but they still designated themselves as catechumens and were frightened away so greatly in the vice of dread that they would not go down to the bath of salvation. Therefore, in this way, those ones were rejected. But those second ones come "to the water" so that there they may be tested. And let us see how they are tested. It is said, "And the Lord said to Gideon: 'Everyone who laps up the water with his tongue as a dog laps, you will set him apart; and everyone who bends his knees so that he may drink, you will transfer[38] him across.' And

---

32. Cf. Rom 12.19.
33. Mt 10.23.
34. Cf. Jgs 7.3.
35. Cf. Rv 21.8.
36. Cf. Jgs 7.3.
37. Jgs 7.4.
38. The term here for "transfer across," *transfero*, can also be translated as "direct" or "bring across."

it happened," it is said, that "the number of those who lapped up the water with his hand or tongue was 300 men, but all the rest bent their knees so that they could drink the water. And the Lord said to Gideon: 'With those 300 men who lapped I will save you all and will hand over Midian into your hand.'"[39]

In nearly all war exploits of the ancestors, great mysteries are signified just as even in this passage we see it happen that those who go down to the water, that is, those who come to the grace of baptism, must not fall prostrate onto the ground nor bend knees and yield to the temptations[40] that are to come along, but, rather, must stand bravely and firmly as even the prophet also said: "Raise up your feeble hands and weak knees,"[41] and, "Make the way straight for your paths."[42] You have come to the water of baptism, that is, to the beginning of the struggle and spiritual battle. Hence, for you the beginning of the battle against the Devil is born. If you would be more relaxed, if you could be made to kneel easily, how will you fight, how will you stand firm against the tricks of the Devil? Therefore, even the Apostle shouts out: "'Therefore, stand firm and refuse to cling again to the yoke of servitude,"[43] and, again, he says: "Stand firm in the Lord,"[44] and, thirdly, he says: "Because now we live if you stand firm in the Lord."[45] Therefore, he is proven, he is elected, who, after he has come to the waters of baptism, does not know to be bent down before earthly and bodily forces; he does not yield to vices, nor does he make himself prostrate, inclined toward a thirst for sin.

Moreover, that he tells them "to lap the water with the hand or the tongue"[46] does not seem to me to be written without a certain force of mystery, namely, that the soldiers of Christ must work with the hand and the tongue, that is, by deed and by

---

39. Jgs 7.5–7.
40. Note that the Latin term here for "temptations," *tentatio*, can mean "temptation" or "attack," which suggests that temptations are attacks or assaults on the soul by the vices and their proponents: the demons and Satan.
41. Heb 12.12; Is 35.3.
42. Heb 12.13. Origen attributed the Epistle to the Hebrews to Paul's authorship.
43. Gal 5.1. 44. Phil 4.1.
45. 1 Thes 3.8. 46. Jgs 7.5–6.

word, because "he who teaches *and* puts into practice, this one will be called great in the kingdom of heaven."[47] But, still, the fact that Scripture proposed a resemblance to a lapping dog,[48] that animal, it seems to me, is named here in the passage because, more than all other animals, he is said to keep the love of his own master, such that neither by time nor by unjust punishments is the affection held within him blotted out.[49]

Therefore, only the 300 men who prefigured the image of this mystery,[50] those chosen, those proven, those consecrated for victory, also were able, by the very mystery of the number, to take possession of the enemies. For indeed the 300 are they who multiply one hundred times three and exhibit the number of the perfect Trinity,[51] under which number census is taken of the whole army of Christ, in which army we should wish that we also may be worthy to be included.

Yet, how do those ones fight? It is said, they carry "jugs[52] and lamps[53] and horned war-trumpets in their hands,"[54] and, it is said, in this way they come to those innumerable multitudes of enemies among whom there were "as many camels as the sand of the sea."[55] And when they had come to war, it is said "they sounded the horned war-trumpets." And they let fall from their hands the "jugs," and "they were crumbled into small pieces."[56] But then, having seized their lamps, they rush forward upon the enemies, and at the same time they sound the war-trumpets. See how the chosen soldiers of God fight with lamps.[57] For Christ had armed them in this way, saying: "Let your loins be girded and your oil-lamps[58] be burning,"[59] and again, "Let your light so

---

47. Mt 5.19. Emphasis added.
48. The term for "proposed" here is a form of *pono*.
49. The term for "blotted out" here, *obliterari*, can also be translated as "canceled."
50. The Latin term for "mystery" here is *sacramentum*.
51. Cf. *Hom in Gn* 2.5.
52. The term for "jugs," *hydria*, can also be translated as "water-pots."
53. The term for "lamps," *lampada*, can also be translated as "torches."
54. Cf. Jgs 7.16. 55. Cf. Jgs 7.12.
56. Cf. Jgs 7.19–20. 57. Ibid.
58. Here the term for "oil-lamp" is *lucerna*.
59. Lk 12.35.

shine before men that they may see your good works and glorify your Father who is in heaven."⁶⁰ Therefore, with such lamps lit up, it is fitting for the soldiers of Christ to fight, shining brightly with the light of works and the brilliance of their deeds.

But what are "the horned war-trumpets" on which "they sound the signal for war"?⁶¹ He who speaks about heavenly things, he who discusses spiritual things, he who lays bare "the mysteries of the kingdom of heaven,"⁶² he it is who sounds⁶³ "the war-trumpet." He speaks of "the war-trumpet" who speaks of noble and very great things, who spreads the knowledge of Christ to human ears. But why is it also called a "horned war-trumpet"? Because it is said even of the saint: "His horn will be exalted in glory."⁶⁴ Whence also the "war-trumpet" of every single person is called "horned" for this reason: that it discusses the manifold knowledge of Christ and the mysteries of his cross, which is designated in the horn. Therefore, being soldiers with this "war-trumpet" and fighting with it, we conquer foreigners and put enemies to flight, even if "their multitude" should be "as numerous as locusts."⁶⁵ For the multitude of demons has been compared to locusts, for whom there is a dwelling-place neither in heaven nor on the earth.

Therefore, in this war may the light of works, the power of knowledge, and the proclamation of the Divine Word lead the way also for us. Let us also fight, singing together in "hymns and psalms and spiritual songs"⁶⁶ and "calling out to God,"⁶⁷ so that we may be worthy to obtain victory in Christ Jesus our Lord from him himself, "to whom are glory and dominion forever and ever. Amen."⁶⁸

---

60. Mt 5.16.
61. Jgs 7.19–22.
62. Mt 13.11.
63. The term for "sounds" here, a form of *concino*, can also be translated as "plays" and can mean "sings prophetically," and, hence, "prophesies."
64. Ps 111.9 (112.9). The term here for "glory," *gloria*, can also be translated as "honor."
65. Cf. Jgs 7.12 and 6.5.
66. Cf. Col 3.16.
67. Cf. Jgs 6.7.
68. 1 Pt 4.11.

INDICES

GENERAL INDEX

Abiezer, Abiezrites, 103, 103n27
Abinoam, 92
Adam: fall of, 101n9
advent: of Christ, 92, 106
adverse powers, 95. *See also* demons
Ahaz, 40, 40n10
aids: human, 111
allegory. *See* Scripture
altar, altars, 54, 63, 98–99, 105
Amalek, Amalekites, 34n127, 67, 95, 100–103
ambidextrous, 67–68, 70–71
Ambrose of Milan, 4n5
Ammonites, 67
anagogical sense. *See* Scripture
anatole, 101n9
ancestors, 106, 116
ancient, the ancients, 46–47, 46n40, 47n50, 114
angel, angels, 26–30, 26n70, 34, 42, 42n22, 64–65, 65n31, 68–69, 79, 85n11, 85–87, 99, 101n9, 104, 107; savior-angels, 64–65; destroyer angel(s), 69, 86–87; angels of darkness, 42n22, 107; angel(s) of light, 28, 42, 42n22, 44, 107
animal man, 32, 74–75, 75n41, 80, 80n28, 82–83, 83n46
anthropology: of Origen, 59n65, 75, 88–89, 89n44, 90n58, 91–92, 91n68, 92n72
Apostle, the, 45, 51–54, 57–58, 67, 76, 81, 83, 93, 95, 108, 114, 116. *See also* Paul
apostle, apostles, 27, 39n3, 43n26, 44n27, 46, 48, 50, 59, 108

apostolic, 23, 31n104, 33n125, 46, 83, 87, 105
apostolic authority, 59
Apostolic Tradition, 22n63, 22n65, 23n66
Aquinas, 3, 3n3
army: of Christ, 112–14, 117
ascend, ascent, 27, 28n84, 32–33, 32n111, 62, 78–80, 96, 99, 103, 103n21
Ashtaroth, 58–59
astrologers, 57
Assyrians, 69
audience: of Origen, 4–5, 13, 15, 15n37, 16n42, 16n45, 18–19, 18–19n54, 20–24, 27–30, 28n84, 31n106, 68, 85, 96n12, 109, 109n72, 109n74; of preacher generally, 109n72; of Rufinus, 6, 6n11, 6n12, 8–11, 12n28. *See also* hearer, hearers; listener, listeners; pupil; disciple, disciples
Augustine, 3

Baal, Baals, Baalim, 28, 54–55, 58–59, 61, 63
Babylon, king of: as figure of Satan, 101n9
Baehrens, W. A., 35, 35n134, 35n135
Balthasar, H. Urs von, 4n5
banquet: wedding, 110
baptism: of water, 19, 22, 22n64, 22n65, 23, 28n84, 31, 97–98, 97–98n27, 116; of blood, 19, 28, 97–99, 97–98n27, 99n38; second baptism by death, 19, 98; as bath of salvation, 115; spiritual

121

baptism: spiritual baptism *(cont.)* baptism, 31–32; as water of the Scriptures, 32, 109, 109n72
Barak, 32–34, 76, 77n11, 78–79, 81, 83, 84–85, 84–85n6, 92; as the first people, 78–79, 81, 83, 85
Bardy, G., 7n15, 105n37
Bartholomew: the Apostle, 46
Basilides, 43n26
basin, 31, 104, 108–9
battles: generally, 87, 92–93, 112–13; for the soul, 19, 20–22, 26, 26n70, 27–32, 34, 87, 92, 113, 116; divine battles, 111; human battles, 111; spiritual battles, 116
Belial, 45
belief, 25, 33–34, 84–85n6, 97, 101n9. *See also* unbelief, disbelief
believe, believers, 10–12, 12n28, 14–15, 17, 16–17n46, 18n54, 19–21, 24, 24n67, 26–28, 28n84, 29–31, 32n111, 33, 35, 42, 45, 47, 50, 53–56, 77, 77n11, 102, 107–8, 109n74. *See also* unbeliever, unbelievers, nonbeliever, nonbelievers
Benedict XVI, Pope (Joseph Ratzinger), 3–4n4
Benjamin, 67
Bethel, 76, 78
Blackman, E. C., 44n27
bless, 5, 14, 19, 45–46, 81, 85–86, 88–89, 91–92, 97–99
blessing, blessings, 5, 81, 85
blood, 19, 28n84, 81, 87, 92, 97–99, 97–98n27, 99n38
boast, 60, 74, 111
bodily meaning/sense. *See* Scripture
body: generally, 55, 88–89, 89n44, 91–92, 91n68, 92n71, 92n72, 113–14, 114n26; weakness of, 114; bodily forces, 116; bodily enemies, 94; as a beast of burden: 91–92, 92n71, 92n72; body of Christ, 59
Bozrah, 99
Bridegroom: as Christ, 32, 110
bread of life, 87

Bruce, B., 4–5n8, 6n10, 6n12, 8n17, 9n22, 12n28, 18, 18n53, 19, 18–19n54, 19n55, 19n56, 39n2
Caleb, 18, 65
Canaan, Canaanites, 74
Cappadocians, 4n5
captive, captives, 55, 92, 96
captivity, 69, 92
carnal: generally, 45; referring to Israel, 100
Cassian, John, 4n5
catechumens, 22–23, 22n62, 22n64, 22n65, 115
Chadwick, H., 7, 7–8n16
chaff, 34, 107
chains, 63
Chalcedon: Council of, 3n1
Christ, 3n1, 4, 4n7, 4n8, 19–20, 24–28, 24n67, 25n68, 26n71, 28n84, 31–34, 31n106, 32n111, 34–35n133, 39n2, 40–42, 44–45, 48, 50, 51–53, 51n3, 52n9, 55, 57, 59–60, 62–63, 69, 71–72, 72n24, 75, 77n11, 78–79, 81, 81–82n42, 83, 84–85n6, 86n19, 87–88, 90, 92–93, 94, 97–99, 99n38, 101, 105n37, 106, 106n43, 106n44, 106n47, 107–8, 110, 112–18; the name of, 101; as King, 88–89; the coming of, 106, 106n43; laws of, 115; soldiers of, 113, 116, 118; army of, 113–14, 117; spiritual knowledge of Christ, 71; virtues equal to, 4, 28, 28n84, 51n3
Christian, Christians, 3, 3–4n4, 4n5, 6, 9, 13–14, 16, 18–19n54, 22–25, 43–44n26, 44n27, 62, 75n41, 85, 97, 100n4, 105–6, 106n42
Church: universal, 3, 3–4n4, 19, 22–27, 22n64, 24–25n67, 26n71, 32–34, 32n111, 34n127, 34n128, 34–35n133, 43–44n26, 59, 61, 61–62n8, 63, 65–67, 71, 73, 75, 77n11, 80–85, 80n26, 81n40, 81–82n42, 84–85n6, 100n4, 101–2,

GENERAL INDEX 123

101n9; the Jews and the Church, 105n37
Church leader, Church leaders: as in Origen's audience, 21, 21n61, 23, 29n88, 30, 34, 63n23, 65–68. *See also* audience; clergy; teacher teachers, teaching; instructor
circumcision, people of the, 106. *See also* Israel, Israelites; Jews
clean, cleanse: from sin(s), 60, 97, 107–10, 107n60, 109n81
clergy, 63n23
co-disciples, 31, 109, 109n74
confess, confession, 52, 52n12, 64, 92, 96, 115
conscience, 96
conversion, 67–68
courage, courageous, 112, 114
creation, 101n9
cross, 72, 112; Cross of Christ, 31–33, 72, 72n24, 80, 114, 118; the power of the wood as the Cross of Christ, 84
Crouzel, H., 8, 8n18, 8n19, 10n23, 13n31, 14n35, 16, 16n42, 16n43, 16n44, 16n45, 17n47, 43n23, 47–48n52, 89n44, 91n69, 101n9
Cyprian, 9–10n23
Cyrrhus, 34n128, 105n37
Cushanrishathaim, 29, 61–64, 66

Daley, B., 21n61
Damasus, 9–10n23
Daniélou, J., 4n5
darkness: generally, 41–42, 41n13, 45, 63; referring to Gnostic cosmology, 75n41; world of, 93; people of, 100; angels of, 107; referring to the Devil, 28, 42n22. *See also* angel, angels; demon, demons; Devil; Satan; Evil One
David, 77–78; root of, 87
de Faye, E., 7n14
de Lubac, H., 8, 8n19
death, 26, 26n71, 28, 41, 51, 57, 62–63, 66, 81–84, 98, 113

Deborah, 17, 33, 75–79, 77n11, 83–85, 84n4, 84–85n6, 92–93, 93n82, 113; as the figure of prophecy, 75, 77, 77n11, 78–80, 84, 84–85n6, 86, 92, 93n82
Decius, 14, 14n33, 18–20, 18–19n54
deeds: of God, 50; referring to good works, 66, 68, 96, 118. *See also* works
Demetrius, 16n41
demon, demons: generally, 26, 26n70, 27–30, 34, 57, 95, 99, 103, 116n40, 118; as princes, 68; as adverse powers, 95
Devil, 20, 27–28, 30–31, 33, 33n125, 42n22, 44, 44n28, 44–45n30, 45, 49, 55, 59–60, 67–68, 87, 102, 102n18, 116; as ruler of this world, 98. *See also* Satan, the Evil One
dew, 33–34, 104–5, 108; divine dew, 105–7; dew of Moses, 105; heavenly dew, 106, 108; dew of heavenly grace, 31, 108
DeWitt, N. W., 43n23
Didache, 22n63
Dionysius, pseudo-, 4n5
dirty clothes, 110
disbelief, 106
disciple, disciples, 31, 31n106, 53, 72, 72n15, 78, 97, 108, 113
Dively Lauro, E. A., 4n6, 4n7, 21n60 and 21n61, 25n68, 26n69, 32n107, 32n111, 48n53, 51n3, 52n9, 76n4, 77n6, 89n44, 90n58, 103n22, 103n24
Divine Word, 77, 89, 105, 108, 110, 115, 118. *See also* Word of God
divinization, 91n64
dread at heart, 111–13, 115
dualistic views, 43n26

East: as the name of Christ, 100n4, 101, 101n9, 102n11; the people of the, 34n127, 95, 100–103, 100n4; as the name of Satan, 101n9, 102n11

GENERAL INDEX

Eckhart, Meister, 3n3
Eglon, 30, 66–68, 70, 71n9
Egypt, Egyptians, 15–16n41, 25, 49, 55, 68–69, 86–87
Ehud, 30, 64, 67–68, 70–71, 71n9, 73–74
elders, 27, 39, 39n3, 45–48, 50, 54, 54n24
elect, elected, 47, 116
election, 54
Eli: sons of, 48
Elijah, 54
end of time, 25–26, 26n71. *See also* Eschaton
enslavement, 5, 64
Ephraim, Mount, 76
Epicurus, Epicureans, 33, 43n23, 70n7, 80–81, 80n33, 80n34
Erasmus, 3n3
Esau, 81, 81n40
Eschaton, 25. *See also* end of time
eternal fire, 68
eternal life, 43n25, 95
eternity, 32, 42–43, 43n25
Eucharist, 22–23
Eusebius of Caesarea, 4n5, 7n14, 12n28, 13n30, 13n31, 14n35, 15–16, 15n40, 15–16n41, 16–17n46, 17n46, 17–18n50, 20
Evagrius Ponticus, 4n5
evangelical, 70, 83, 105
evil, 27, 29, 40, 42, 43n26, 44n27, 45, 47, 49, 52–54, 60–62, 66–67, 69, 70, 73–74, 82, 94, 112
Evil One: the, 40, 88, 114. *See also* Devil, Satan
exegesis. *See* Scripture
exodus, 11, 12n29, 68, 89
Ezekiel: the prophet, 96

faith, faithful, faithfulness, 13–14, 14n35, 18–19n54, 20, 22, 22n64, 23–25, 41, 43–44n26, 46, 50, 53–54, 62, 63n23, 68, 71, 75n41, 81, 81–82n42, 82–83, 86n19, 87–88, 92, 96–97, 100n4, 101, 101n9, 107, 113–14
fall: of Adam, 101n9; of Satan, 101n9
Father: God the, 9–10n23, 52, 55, 85, 92, 103–4, 118
fear, fearful, 39n3, 41, 56, 111–13, 115. *See also* dread at heart
feet: of the/our soul, 20, 31–32, 31n106, 108–10
feminine mind, 113
Festugière, A. J., 43n23
figure, figures, 29, 64, 72, 75, 78, 80–81, 84, 100n4, 101n9. *See also* Scripture
filth, 108–9, 109n81
firstborn, 69, 81n41, 87
first principles, 33n125, 85–88, 85n10, 86n17, 86n18
fleece, 33–34, 34n128, 104–9, 105n37
flesh, fleshly: generally, 9–10n23, 41, 47, 57, 59, 75, 80, 87–89, 89n44, 92, 92n72, 95, 99; flesh of Israel, 95; fleshly meaning of Scripture, 103
foreign, foreigners, 61, 71, 71n13, 79–81, 83n48, 84, 101n8, 106n48, 118
foreign gods, 58
foreign resident, 71
foreknowledge, 57
foresee, 91n65, 107
foreshadow, 24, 106n43
fountains of Israel, 109
fragrance: of Christ, 63, 63n19
free will. *See* will
fruits of the Spirit, 95–96, 98, 102

garment, garments, 108, 110
Gaza, 95
gentiles, 34, 81, 83, 83n48, 85, 106, 106n48
Gera, 67
Gideon, 30–31, 33–34, 34n127, 34n128, 70n5, 103–7, 103n27, 105n37, 106n49, 111–12, 115–16

GENERAL INDEX 125

Gilead, Mount, 112
glory: to/of God, 31; to/of Christ, 50, 60, 69, 72, 75, 83, 93, 99, 110, 118; of this world, 43, 43n25, 56–57; of the flesh, 80; of prophecy, 84; of the saint, 118, 118n63; glory lost through lack of faith, 74; believer's participation in God's glory, 81, 88
Gnostics, Gnosticism, 43–44n26, 44n27, 75n41
Gordian, 14, 15n37, 16, 17n50
Gospel, Gospels, 22–23, 22n62, 32, 33n125, 43–44n26, 47n27, 46–47, 52, 54, 81, 108, 112; of peace, 110, 114
grace, 20, 31, 28n84, 32n109, 42n20, 54, 62, 75–77, 91n64, 95, 101n9, 107–8, 109n72, 109n73, 116; dew of heavenly grace, 31, 108
grain, 34, 107
Grant, R. M., 43–44n26
Greer, R., 4n5, 14n35, 26n70
Gregory the Great, 4n5
guilt, 88

Hammond, C., 6n9
Hanson, R., 7n14, 7n15, 15n36, 16n42, 17, 17n49
Harnack, A., 44n27
Haroshethhagoiim, 74
harvest, 34, 107
hearer, hearers: of Scripture as part of Origen's audience, 20–21, 23, 25–28, 24–25n67, 31–32, 31n104, 72, 72n15, 76, 85, 89n48, 100, 109n73. *See also* audience, listener
hearing: versus giving ear, 88–90
heart: generally, 28, 42n20, 43, 46, 53, 55–56, 56n43, 58, 60, 68–69, 73, 82, 90–91, 96, 98, 102–3, 109–10, 111–13, 115; clean heart, 110; dread at heart, 111–13, 115
heathenism, 57n48

heaven: generally, 52, 55, 71, 77n12, 80, 85, 92, 98–99, 101n9, 105, 116–18; kingdom of, 117–18
heavenly bread, 87
heavenly dew, 106, 108
heavenly doctrine, 85
heavenly grace: dew of, 31, 108
heavenly host, 64, 68, 87, 107
heavenly promise, 104
heavenly teaching, 77
heavenly things, 45, 80, 118
Hebrew Scriptures, 5, 24–25, 24n67, 39n1. *See also* Old Testament
Heine, R., 5–6n9, 6–7, 6n11, 6n12, 6n13, 7n14, 7n15, 7–8n16, 9n20, 9n21, 9n22, 9–10n23, 10n24, 10n25, 12n28, 12n29, 15n36, 16, 16–17n46, 22n63, 22n64, 22n65, 23n66, 32n111
hemorrhage: the woman with the, 81, 81–82n42
heretics, 3, 9, 9–10n23, 11–12, 12n29, 34n127, 43, 100n4, 101–2, 101n9
high priest: Christ as, 99
Hilary of Poitiers, 4n5, 9–10n23
Hiram, 62, 62n15
historical: sense, meaning, level of meaning in Scripture. *See* Scripture
Hoffmann, R. J., 44n27
Holofernes, 113
holy: elders, 47; Scripture, 48, 82, 89, 96, 108; apostle(s), 50, 83, 108, 114; Church, 63; places, 63; God as the holy one of Israel, 63; work, 96; Gideon, 106, 106n49, 107
Holy Spirit, 9–10n23, 12n29, 71, 107–8
hope, 97, 113
Hoppe, H., 7n14
host, 40, 64, 68, 87, 105, 107
humble, humbles, humbled, 62–64, 92–93
humility, 30, 62–63

GENERAL INDEX

idol, idols, 28–29, 57–58, 61
illumination, 113, 113n19
image, images: to worship, 54, 54n31, 55, 57, 57n50; of God's Spirit, 90n58, 91n68, 114, 114n26; in scriptural interpretation, 68, 84, 117. *See also* Scripture, idol(s)
impassibility: of God, 58
impious, 42, 53–54, 82
impurity, 45, 60, 109, 109n81
Incarnation, 26
inheritance, 50, 64
injustice, 41–42, 45–47, 49, 74, 94
instructor, 86, 86n15, 86n19. *See also* audience; Church leader; clergy; teacher, teachers, teaching
interior man, 89, 91
interior sense. *See* Scripture
interpretation. *See* Scripture
Isaac, 81
Isaiah, 40, 40n10, 109, 116
Israel, Israelites, 4, 5, 18n54, 28–30, 28n78, 29n86, 32–34, 34n127, 34n128, 49, 49n62, 52–54, 58, 61, 63–69, 73–74, 76–77, 79, 81, 85–90, 90n58, 92, 94–95, 100, 101n8, 104–6, 109, 111; people of, 111; leaders of, 85–88; Israel according to the spirit, 94–95; spiritual Israel, 100; flesh of Israel, 95; carnal Israel, 100. *See also* Jews, Synagogue

Jabin, 32, 74, 76
Jacob, 81, 81n40
Jael, 32–34, 33n125, 76, 77n11, 79–81, 83–85, 84n4, 84–85n6
Jaubert, A., 12n28
Jeremiah, 15n36, 109
Jericho, 80n26
Jerome, 4n5, 7n14, 8–9, 9n22, 15n36
Jesus: generally, 3n1, 18n54, 22n64, 27–28, 31–34, 34–35n133, 39, 41, 43n26, 44, 44n27, 45–48, 50, 51–55, 57, 59–60, 69, 72, 75, 77n12, 78, 81–82n42, 83, 84–85n6, 99, 102, 106, 108, 109n73, 110, 112, 115, 118; name of, 4–5, 4–5n8, 18n54, 39n2; days of, 27–28, 39–41, 39n3, 41, 44–45, 47–48, 50; virtues identified with, 4n7, 27–28, 39n3, 48n53, 51n3, 52n9
Jews, 25, 33–34, 34n127, 34–35n133, 59, 77n11, 81, 81–82n42, 84–85n6, 102, 105n37, 106, 106n42; Jewish people, 105; as the first people, 78–79, 81, 83, 94; as the people of God, 84, 88, 92, 102; as the people of the Lord, 94, 101; as the people of the circumcision, 106; Jewish understanding, 103; Jewish tradition of interpretation, 105n37; salvation of, 33, 34–35n133, 77n11, 84–85n6, 85; Jews and the Church, 105n37. *See also* Israel, Israelites; Synagogue
Jezreel, 102
John: the Apostle, 46
Jonas, H. 43–44n26
Joseph, 103n27
Joshua: Jesus son of Nun, 27–28, 51, 65, 107; name of, 4–5n8, 39n2; death of, 28; as successor to Moses, 4–5
Jotham, 40n10
Judah, 40n10
Judges, Homilies on: dating of, 13–20; major themes, 27–34; manuscript history, editions, translations, 35. *See* Origen, writings, *for citations to homilies in introduction and cross-references between the homilies*
judge, judges, 5, 31, 33, 65–66, 67–68, 70–71, 73, 77
judgment, judgments: of Deborah, 76; of God, 58, 61, 65–66, 77, 100
Judith, 113
justice, 40–42, 41n15, 45, 47–49, 52, 63, 66, 92, 96
justification, 53
Justin Martyr: *Apology*, 22n63

GENERAL INDEX

Kenaz, 65–66
kingdom: of heaven, 117–18
knowledge: generally, 43, 43n26, 46, 49n60, 62, 62n16, 76, 97n18, 118; of Christ, 31, 63, 71, 118; the spiritual knowledge of Christ, 71; knowledge of God, 74; word of knowledge, 108; word of the true knowledge, 109, 109n79
Koch, H., 7n14

lamb: the unblemished, 87
Lappidoth, 76
Larsen, L., 26n70
last times, 84, 108
law, laws: generally, 18n54; of Christ, 115; divine/Jewish law, 22, 34, 44, 50, 78, 81, 81–82n42, 88, 100, 104; as divine legislation, 105; law of sin, 55; laws of allegory, 100
Lawson, R. P., 17n47, 17–18n50, 48n53
Layton, B., 43n26, 75n41
leader, leaders: Church, 3, 4n5, 20–21, 21n61, 23, 28, 29n88, 30, 34, 63n23, 65–66, 73, 85, 86, 88; of Israel, 66–67, 73, 81, 85–88, 105; leader of the people, 73; Roman, 14, 18n54; Gnostic, 43–44n26; foreign, 32, 74, 79; as man of God, 73; Christ as the leader of our army, 112; as a savior, 28n78; as demons, 64; as angels, 68, 86–88, 107; as Epicureanism, 70
LeBoulluec, A., 43–44n26
lectio divina, 3–4n4, 4n5
Leemans, J., 26n70, 65n31
left: as in sinister or wrong, 67–69
Leonides: father of Origen, 13
letter of Scripture, 66, 77; letter and spirit of Scripture, 103. *See also* Scripture
levels: of meaning in Scripture, 20, 26, 33, 34n128, 77n6, 89n48; of spiritual growth, 20, 89n48; of spiritual combat, 26n70. *See also* Scripture
levitical, 63
life, 3, 4n5, 26n70, 26n71, 41, 43n23, 43n25, 52–54, 54n28, 57, 59n65, 69, 82, 87, 98, 112–13, 112n13, 113n20
light: true (relating to Christ), 27, 39–40, 40n6, 42, 44–46; light of Christ, 44; eternal light, 28, 42; light of the world, 42, 46; light of sanctification, 45; people of the light (referring to Christians), 100n4; light of the just, 42; light of works, 118; angel(s) of light, 28, 42, 42n22, 44, 107; light versus darkness, 45; light of the impious/wicked, 42; fleeting/false light (referring to the Devil/to be extinguished), 28, 40, 42–44; light contrary to the truth, 40; impermanent light of the first chosen people of God, 33, 78; light of knowledge, 46; light in Gnostic cosmology, 75n41
listener: in Origen's audience, 64, 72n15, 82, 109. *See also* hearer, audience
literal sense/meaning. *See* Scripture
liturgy, 22
locusts, 111, 118
Logan, A., 43–44n26
Lord of Hosts, 40
love, 42, 46, 50, 56n42, 55–58, 87, 90, 117
Lubac, H. de, 8, 8n19
Lucifer, 101n9, 102n11. *See also* Devil, Satan, Evil One, East
Luther, Martin, 3n3

mammon, 56–57
man of God, 73. *See also* leader
Manasseh: 7th-century king of Judah, 40; tribe of Israel, 103n27
manna, 49
Marcion, 43–44, 43–44n26, 44n27

Markschies, C., 43–44n26
marriage chamber, 32, 110
Martens, P., 24–25n67
martyr, 98
martyrdom: physical, 14, 19, 28n84, 97–98, 97–98n27, 99, 99n38, 114; spiritual, 14, 19, 28n84
material world, 43–44n26, 44n27, 75n41
Maximin the Thracian, 13–15, 15n37
Maximus the Confessor, 4n5
McGuckin, J., 3n2, 24–25n67, 65n31
meaning. *See* Scripture
medicine, 29, 61
meditate, meditation, 85, 106
mercy, 29–30, 42n20, 47, 63–64, 66, 68
merit, 73, 77, 98
Mesopotamia, 29, 61–62
Messiah, 100n4, 101n9, 106n42
method: Origen's method of Scriptural interpretation, 21n61, 24–27. *See also* Scripture
Midian, Midianites, 30–31, 34n127, 70, 70n5, 94–96, 98, 100–103, 111, 116
military: camp, 103n25, 113, 115; equipment, 113; supports, 113; offense, 115
milk: as spiritual food, 33n125, 82–83, 87
mind, minds, 41, 47–48n52, 56, 56n42, 56n43, 58–60, 58n57, 59n62, 59n65, 58n57, 69, 69n62, 74n33, 75, 75n51, 77, 88n43, 89–90, 90n58, 90n60, 91, 91n66, 91n69, 96, 96n14, 101, 101n6, 112, 112n9, 113, 113n16, 113n22, 113n25, 114, 114n26; feminine mind, 113
Moab, Moabites, 30, 66–68, 70n5
moral instruction, 82
Moser, M., 9–10n23, 12n29
Moses, 5, 50, 69, 86; dew of Moses, 105

Murphy, F., 5–6n9, 6n11, 6n12, 9, 9n21, 18, 18n53, 19
mystery, mysteries, 31, 76–77, 79–80, 82, 84–85, 85n10, 87, 105–6, 116–17, 117n50, 118
mystical understanding/type. *See* Scripture

Nautin, P., 7n15, 13n30, 13n31, 15–18, 15n36, 15n37, 15n38, 15n39, 16–17n46, 17n48, 17n50, 18n51, 18n52, 18–19n54, 22–23, 22n63, 23n66
New Testament, 24–25, 31n104, 35, 106n49. *See also* Gospel, Gospels; Scripture
Nicaea: Council of, 3n1
Noah, 32n111
numbers: mystery of (senary), 72

O'Keefe, J., 24–25n67
Old Testament, 16–17n46, 22–24, 22n62, 35, 44n27. *See also* Hebrew Scriptures, Scripture
Origen: life of, 13–14; declared a heretic, 3, 3n2; method of allegorical interpretation, 24–27
Origen: writings,
 —*De principiis*,
  generally: 25;
  1.2: 9–10n23;
  1.3: 9–10n23, 10n24;
  1.8.1: 65n31, 85n11;
  2.9.5: 43–44n26;
  3: 9–10n23, 10n25;
  3.1.10: 42n20;
  3.4: 89n44;
  4: 20–21, 21n61, 25–26, 26n69, 103n22, 103n24;
 —*Exhortation to Martyrdom*,
  generally: 14;
  30: 97n23;
 —*Commentary on Song of Songs*,
  prologue: 17, 17n47;
  1: 52n9;
  1.2: 63n20;

GENERAL INDEX

1.5: 4n7, 48n53, 51n3;
—*Commentary on John,*
32.4–18: 108n69
—*Commentary on Romans,*
generally: 7, 7–8n16, 9–10n23, 10–11
—*Homilies on Song of Songs,*
generally: 17–18n50, 18;
1.1: 77n8, 85n8;
2.6: 63n20
—*Homilies on Genesis,*
2: 21n60, 26n69 and 32n111;
2.5: 117n51;
11: 12n29, 21n60 and 26n69;
11.3: 16n45;
12: 12n29 and 81n40
—*Homilies on Leviticus,*
2.2.7: 89n44;
5: 21n60, 26n69;
11: 12n29;
13.5.1: 72n23
—*Homilies on Numbers,*
9: 21n60, 26n69;
11: 12n29;
11.4: 65n31;
25.1: 102n11;
27: 27n72;
27.11–12: 107n56
—*Homilies on Joshua,*
generally: 4–5n8, 5–6n9, 11, 12n28, 19–20, 39n2;
1.7: 19n56;
3.4–5: 80n26;
4: 22n62, 22n64 and 19n54;
5.1: 18–19n54;
9: 18–19, 18n54, 22n62;
10.1: 19n56;
10.3: 19n56;
14.2: 74n34;
15.3: 74n34;
18–20: 18, 19n55, 65n33;
20: 12n28;
20.3–6: 18, 65n33;
21.1: 19n56;
—*Homilies on Judges* (cross-references between homilies),

1: 54n24;
1.1: 40n10, 70n7, 80n33;
1.3: 51n3;
1.4: 62, 62n16;
2: 61n2;
3.3: 18;
3.4: 73n26;
3.6: 87n23;
4.4: 80n27, 80n28, 80n29;
4.4–5: 84n3;
5: 93;
5.3: 84–85n6;
5.4–6: 84n3;
9.1: 77n7;
—*Homilies on Judges* (references in Introduction),
generally: 19;
1: 27–28;
1.1: 27n73;
1.2: 31n104;
1.3: 4n7, 28n76;
2: 28–29, 28n77;
2.1: 28n80;
2.2–5: 28n83;
2.3: 28n79;
2.5: 28n78, 29n88, 29n89, 30n93;
3: 29–30, 29n85;
3.1: 29n86;
3.1–3.2: 29n88;
3.2–3.3: 29n90, 30n94;
3.3: 18, 26n70, 28n78, 29n87, 29n89, 29n90, 29n91, 29n92, 30n93;
3.4: 28n78, 30n93;
3.4–3.6: 26n70;
3.5: 30n95;
3.6: 29n89, 30n96;
4: 32–33;
4.2: 30n97, 30n98, 30n99;
4.4: 32n112, 32n113;
5: 32–33;
5.2: 33n116, 33n117;
5.4: 33n114, 33n115, 33n118, 33n119, 33n121;
5.5: 32n113, 33n120, 33n122,

Origen: writings, *Homilies on Judges* (cont.)
   33n123, 33n124, 33n125, 34–35n133;
   5.6: 21n60, 33n125;
   6.2: 21n60, 26n70;
   7: 19, 28n84;
   7.1–7.2: 26n70;
   7.2: 19n57, 19n58, 28n84;
   8: 31–34; 32n109;
   8.1: 34n127;
   8.4: 34n126, 34n128, 34n130, 34n131, 34n132;
   8.5: 20, 31n105, 31n106, 32n108, 32n109, 32n110, 34n129;
   9: 30–31;
   9.1: 30n100;
   9.2: 31n101–3;
   —*Homilies on Psalms,* 11
   —*Homilies on Jeremiah,* 15n36
   —*Homilies on Luke,*
   generally: 22n65;
   11.3: 89n44;
   21.4, 22.8 and 32.5: 22n62
Othniel, 29–30, 64–66
Oulton, J., 7n14, 12n28

pagans, paganism, 34n127, 57, 102
Pamphilus: *Defense of/Apology for Origen,* 6n10, 7n15, 16–17n46
passion, passions, 32, 56–58, 56n42, 58n56, 60
Passion of Christ, 19
Paul: the Apostle, 44n27, 46, 48, 51, 51n5, 57, 63, 76, 87, 95, 116. *See also* Apostle, the
peace: during Origen's life, 13–14, 15n37, 16, 19; for Israel, 28, 64, 66, 94; for believers, 41–42; of Christ's time, 41; of Christ, 41; Gospel of, 110, 114
people of God, 33, 84, 88, 92, 101–2. *See also* Jews; Israel, Israelites
perfection: spiritual, 22n64, 25
Perkins, P., 43–44n26

persecute, persecution: generally, 75, 96, 102, 114–15; during Origen's life, 13–20
Peter: the Apostle, 46, 51, 108
Pharaoh, 40, 40n9, 62, 68
Philip the Arabian, 14, 16
Philistines, 30, 71–72, 79
Philocalia, 8, 9–10n23, 12n28
philosophers, 57
philosophy, 13, 70, 70n7, 71, 80–81, 80n33, 80n34
pleasure, pleasures, 33, 43, 43n23, 56–57, 59, 70, 70n7, 80–81, 80n33, 96
pneumatic: sense/meaning. *See* Scripture
power: of Christ, 26, 93, 99, 99n38; of God, 30–31, 69, 111; divine/ of the angels, 29, 57, 65, 68, 98; of the demons, 57, 64, 67, 93, 95, 96–97; of Scripture, 31; of the Cross, 33, 80, 84; of church leaders, 59, 73; of the Devil, 59, 94; of this world, 62, 111; of Israel's leaders, 91; in battle, 92; of Israel's enemies, 94–95; against the Church generally, 97; of the Church/believers collectively, 97; of individual believers, 109n78; of faith, 113; of the mind, 113; of knowledge, 118
praise, praises, 70, 92
pray, prayer: generally, 3–4n4, 28, 31, 45, 55, 73, 97, 108; weapons of, 114
preacher: role of, 20–21, 21n61, 30–32, 32n109, 34, 109n72, 109n73
prefigured, 117
pride: 29, 52, 62–64, 69, 101n9. *See also* proud
priest, priests, priestly, 22n64, 59, 63, 88
primacy: as first place, 33, 77n11, 79, 81, 83, 84–85n6
primogeniture, 81, 81n41
promise, promises: of God, 104, 111
prophecy, prophecies: general, 40,

75, 77, 77n11, 78–80, 84–85, 84–85n6, 86, 92–93, 93n82, 118n62; figured by Deborah, 75, 77, 77n11, 78–80, 84, 84n6, 86, 92; prophetic grace, 77, 77n11, 93, 93n82, 118; prophetic spirit, 106; prophetic word, 71, 99; prophetic, heavenly signs, 49; prophetic portents, 104; to sing prophetically, 118n62
prophet, prophets, prophetess: generally, 16–17n46, 31, 33, 41–42, 54, 76–77, 84–85n6, 96, 105, 108, 118; referring to Isaiah, 40, 116; referring to Ezekiel, 96; writings of the prophets, 105
protector, 113
proud, 62–63, 74. *See also* pride
providence, 61, 61–62n8
pseudo-Dionysius, 4n5
psychic: sense/meaning. *See* Scripture
punishment, 63–64, 67; unjust, 117
pupil, pupils, 72n15, 82, 86, 86n14
purified, 110

Rahab, 80n26
rain, rains, raindrops, 42n20, 106
Ramah, 76, 78
Ramses, 40n9
rational: part of the soul, 88n43, 90n58, 91n69, 113n22, 113n25, 114n26
Rebecca: mother of Esau and Jacob, 81
redemption, 97
Red Sea, 25, 86
renounce, 72, 113
repentance, repenting, repentant, 5, 28n78, 29–30, 51, 64, 68; unrepentant, 58
resurrection, 9–10n23, 12n29, 24–25n67, 26
righteous, righteousness, 76, 78, 81, 92, 94, 114
right-handed, 67–69
Robinson, J., 7–8, 8n17, 9–10n23, 12n28

Rudolph, K., 43–44n26
Rufinus of Aquileia: as translator, 4n8, 5–12, 5–6n9, 6n11, 7n14, 7n15, 7–8n16, 9–10n23, 12n28, 12n29, 15n36, 23–24, 47n46, 47n47, 47–48n52, 49n62, 67n45, 77n11, 84–85n6, 89n45, 93n82, 97–98n27, 99n38, 101n8; reliability as a translator, 5–9; method of translation, 9–12; *Apology against Jerome* 2.40, 9n22; preface to *De principiis*, 10n24, 10n25; preface to *Homilies in Joshua*, 19n55; preface and epilogue to *Commentary on Romans*, 9–10n23, 10n24, 10n25, 10–11, 11n26, 11n27, 12n28
ruler of this world, rulers of this world: referring to Satan or the demons, 93, 98

sacrament, sacraments, sacramental, 32n109, 109n72, 109n73
sacramentum, 117n50
sacrifice, 92, 105; divine sacrifices, 98
sages, 80, 106
saints, 46, 52, 68, 118
salvation: generally, 5, 25–26, 28n84, 29n88, 32–34, 40, 43–44n26, 47, 50, 64, 68, 77n11, 80n26, 81, 84–85n6, 85, 87, 99n38, 100n4, 104–6, 113–14, 116; bath of (referring to baptism), 115; of Israel, 33–34, 68, 77n11; attained in Church alone, 80n26; of Israel with Church at end of time, 54, 81, 85
Satan, 44–45n30, 59–60, 69, 101n9, 102n18, 116n40. *See also* Devil, Evil One, Tyre
Saul, 73
save, 5, 30, 33, 34–35n133, 54, 59, 64, 67, 75n41, 81, 85, 104–5, 111, 116
Savior: as Jesus Christ, 35, 41, 46, 49, 54, 108, 112

savior, saviors, 28n78, 29, 29n89, 30, 64, 67–68
Scheck, T., 9–10n23, 10n24
Scherer, J., 7–8n16
Scripture:
 allegory/allegorical(ly): generally, 20–21, 24–25n67, 26n71, 39n3, 77n11, 82, 84–85n6, 100, 106n43, 106n44, 106n47; versus typology, 24–25n67;
 anagogical sense, 26n71;
 baptismal function, 31–32;
 bodily sense/meaning, 25, 89, 89n45, 103n22;
 exegesis, 3, 5, 9, 21, 25, 24–25n67, 26n71, 27, 103; Origen's method of, 24–27; medieval exegesis, 26n71;
 fleshly meaning, 103;
 historical: sense in Scripture, 26n71; meaning in Scripture, 103n22;
 interaction with, 31–34, 32n109, 33n125;
 interior sense, 77;
 interpretation(s), 5, 20, 21n61, 24, 24–25n67, 35, 105n37
 Jewish tradition of interpretation, 105n37. See also Jews;
 Jewish understanding, 103. See also Jews;
 letter, 66, 77; letter and spirit, 103;
 levels of meaning, 20, 26, 33, 34n128, 77n6, 89n48;
 literal sense/meaning, 20–21, 24–26, 24–25n67, 26n71, 27n72, 76n4, 77n6, 103n24;
 meaning in, 8–9, 12n29, 20, 24–25n67, 25–26, 25n68, 26n69, 33, 34n128, 67, 71, 76n4, 77n6, 77n11, 89n45, 89n48, 101, 102n11, 103, 103n22, 103n24, 109, 109n77, 112, 112n11;
 method: Origen's method of Scriptural interpretation, 21n61, 24–27;
 mystical understanding, 82, 85; mystical type, 84;
 pneumatic (spiritual) sense, 20–21, 26–27, 26n71, 32–34, 34n128, 76n4, 77n6, 77n11, 84–85n6, 103n24, 105n37;
 psychic (soul's) sense, 20–21, 26–29, 26n71, 28n84, 29n86, 31–34, 76n7, 77n6;
 sense(s) of meaning, 20–21, 25–27, 25n68, 26n69, 26n71, 29, 64, 76n4, 77, 89n45, 103n24;
 somatic (bodily/literal) sense, 25–26;
 spirit of Scripture, 103;
 spiritual meaning(s)/sense(s)/understanding, 26, 64, 67–68, 76n4, 77n6, 103, 103n24, 105n37;
 tropology, 26n71;
 typology, 34n128; versus allegory, 24–25, 24–25n67;
 water(s) of Scripture, 32, 108–9, 109n72, 109n73.
 See also figure, figures; image, images; type, types
seed: of God, 102
senary, 72. See also numbers
Sennacherib, 69
sense, senses: of meaning. See Scripture
Septimius Severus, 13, 15–16n41
Septuagint (LXX), 35, 39n1, 41n13, 89n54, 92n77, 92n80, 93n83, 101n9
shadows, 108
Shamgar, 30, 70–72, 74
sign, signs, 33–34, 49, 104–7
sin, sins, sinning, sinful, 5, 14, 19–20,

GENERAL INDEX   133

28–30, 28n78, 28n84, 29n89, 32, 49, 51–55, 58–60, 62, 64, 66–67, 69, 72–73, 90, 94–96, 98, 100, 107n60, 109, 116; after baptism, 97–98

sinner, sinners, 29n86, 33n125, 43, 51–53, 59

Sisera, 32–33, 33n125, 74, 75n41, 76, 77n11, 79–83, 84, 84–85n6

slavery, 67, 69; satanic slavery, 69

Socrates: *Church History*, 22n63

soldier, soldiers, 111–14, 118; of/for God, 114, 117; of Christ, 113, 116, 118

Solomon, 78

somatic sense. *See* Scripture

Son: God's only, 50

Son of God, 9–10n23, 51, 102n11, 106, 108

Son of man, 46

songs: in the Scriptures, 89–90

soul, souls, 19–20, 26–32, 26n70, 40–42, 47, 47–48n52, 55, 55n39, 56, 56n43, 56n45, 58, 59n65, 60, 60n71, 62, 66, 66n37, 72, 75, 75n41, 75n51, 83, 83n46, 86n19, 88n43, 89n44, 90, 90n58, 90n61, 91–92, 91n68, 91n69, 92n73, 94, 94n3, 96–99, 108–9, 109n72, 112n9, 112n13, 113n22, 113n25, 114n26, 116n40; feet of the/our soul, 108–10

spirit: generally, 56n43, 59, 59n65, 60, 75, 75n41, 88–89, 88n43, 89n44, 90, 90n58, 91n68, 94–96, 95n9, 112n9, 113n25, 114, 114n26; referring to the demons, 60; spirits of wickedness, 93; Israel according to the spirit, 94–95; spiritual Israel, 100; prophetic spirit, 106; letter and spirit of Scripture, 103

Spirit: of God, 9–10n23, 12n29, 65–66, 71, 87, 90n58, 91n68, 102–3, 107–8, 114, 114n26

spiritual: battles, 116; growth, 4, 96n12; man, 74–75, 75n41, 107; things, 118; enemies, 94; caution, 107; levels of spiritual advancement or preparedness, 89n48; spiritual meaning(s)/sense(s), understanding in Scripture, 26, 64, 67–68, 76n4, 77n6, 103, 103n24, 105n37

Strutwolf, H., 43–44n26

Studer, B., 7n14

suffer, 5, 29, 73, 81, 95, 105–6, 106n40

Sun of Justice, 40–41, 100n4

Synagogue, 81, 81n40, 81–82n42. *See also* Jews; Israel, Israelites

Syrians, 57

Tabor, Mount, 33, 79

teachers, teaching: generally, 3–4n4, 13, 20–21, 21n61, 31, 48, 58, 63, 63n23, 71, 76–78, 83, 86, 86n13, 86n16, 86n19, 95, 109n79, 116; Christ as the Teacher, 25, 25n68, 32, 46, 86, 86n19, 109. *See also* pupil, instructor

temptation, temptations, 46–47, 101n9, 116, 116n40

Tertullian, 22n63

testing God, 104

Theodoret, 34n128, 105n37

Thompson, F., 26n70

thought, thoughts, 60, 69n62, 112; evil, 53, 60

threshing floor, 33–34, 104, 107–8

Timothy, 53

Torjesen, K. J., 21n61, 25n68, 32n107

transgression, transgressions, 59

transgressors, 63, 66

Trigg, J., 3n2, 14n35

Trinity, 3n1, 7n15, 9, 9–10n23, 12n29, 117

tropology. *See* Scripture

truth, truths, 21n60, 25, 24–25n67, 27, 27n72, 31, 31n106, 33, 33n125, 40, 45, 52, 69, 71, 114

type, types, 4n8, 14, 24–25, 24–25n67, 27, 29, 31, 33, 34n127, 39n2, 80n26, 84, 105n37. *See also* Scripture
typology. *See* Scripture
tyranny, 114; tyrannous, 114; tyrant Eglon, 70
Tyre, Prince of, 62n15; as figure of Satan, 101n9

unbelief, 34
unbeliever, unbelievers, nonbeliever, nonbelievers, 45, 54
unchangeability: of God, 58
uncleanness, 109n81
unfaithful, 115
universal: faith, 101, 101n10
unrighteousness, 92
Uzziah, 40, 40n10

Valentinus, Valentinian, Valentinians, 43n26, 75n41
valley, valleys, 102–3
Venus, 57
vice, vices, 5, 20–22, 26, 26n70, 27–31, 34, 57–58, 60, 62–63, 67, 72, 80–81, 83, 89, 109, 112, 115–16, 116n40
victory, 30–31, 79–81, 83, 84–85, 84n4, 111, 114, 117–18
vine: true, 87
virgins, 114
virtue, virtues: generally, 14, 18–19n54, 19–22, 26–32, 26n70, 28n84, 31n104, 43n23, 47–48, 51n3, 52–53, 52n9, 70n7, 75n41, 80n33, 88, 96–97; as identified with Jesus Christ, 4, 4n7, 39n3, 48n53, 51n3, 52n9
vision, visions, 32, 40, 40n10, 74–75, 74n40, 80, 107
Völker, W., 7n15

Wagner, M., 6n11, 6n12, 9, 9n20, 12n28
war, wars: generally, 31, 66, 84, 92, 103, 111, 113, 116–18; spiritual (battle for soul against demons and vices), 26n70, 41–42, 87, 101, 114, 118
wash: clean of sins, 20, 28n84, 108–10, 109n72; wash feet of soul, 31–32, 109n73
water, waters: of Scripture, 32, 108–9, 109n72, 109n73. *See also* baptism, Scripture
weakness, weaknesses, weaken: human, 53, 62, 92–93, 96, 112; of gender, 77, 114; of the body, 114; of the Devil, 67
weapons: of prayer, 114; spiritual, 114
wedding banquet, 110
West: the people of the, 100–101. *See also* East, the people of the
wicked, wickedness, 27, 39–42, 40n10, 45, 53, 58, 66–67, 74; spirits of, 93
will: as in human/free, 42n20, 64, 74, 86, 88, 96; of God, 73–74
Wilson, R. S., 44n27
wisdom, 45, 47, 78; of God, 80
woman, women, 32, 76–81, 81–82n42, 83–84, 113–14
Word of God, 34, 71, 73, 77n11, 84–85n6, 85, 88–89, 91, 102–3, 105, 108, 110; as the word of knowledge, 108. *See also* Divine Word
works: of God, 48–50, 52, 90n58; works of life in the soul, 52–53; good works, 53–54, 58, 92, 96, 117–18. *See also* deeds
wrath of God, 58, 61

INDEX OF HOLY SCRIPTURE

Old Testament

Genesis
  27.5–29: 81

Exodus
  1.8–14: 40on9
  1.11: 62
  1.14: 68
  2.23: 68
  3.9: 68–69
  6.6: 49
  10.1–20: 111
  11.4: 69
  11.7: 87
  12.21–30: 69
  12.23–29: 87
  12.42: 55
  13.3: 49
  14.14: 86
  14.19: 86
  14.21: 49
  15.1–21: 89
  16: 49
  19.3: 49–50
  24.12: 50
  32.9: 74

Numbers
  21.17–18: 89

Deuteronomy
  5.15: 49
  6.5: 55–56
  6.16: 104

18.15: 75
20.1–4: 111–12
32.1–43: 89

Joshua
  5.13–14: 107
  17.2: 103n27

Judges
  2–3: 29–30
  2.7: 27, 39–50
  2.8: 28, 51–52, 54
  2.10: 52–54
  2.11: 52, 54
  2.11–12: 54–55
  2.12: 58
  2.12–14: 58–59
  2.14: 61
  3.7: 61–62
  3.8: 61–64, 66–67
  3.9: 64–65
  3.10: 65–66
  3.11: 66
  3.12: 66–67
  3.12–13: 67
  3.14: 67
  3.15: 64, 67–68, 70
  3.15–16: 68
  3.17–25: 70–71
  3.31: 70–72
  4: 30, 32–33
  4.1: 73–74
  4.2: 74, 76

4.3: 74–75, 84
4.4: 75–76, 113
4.4–5: 76–78
4.6: 78–79
4.8: 79
4.9: 79–81, 83–84
4.14–22: 79–85
5: 77n11, 84
5.2: 85–88
5.2–31: 89
5.3: 88–90
5.6–15: 83
5.9: 90
5.9–10: 91–92
5.11 (LXX): 92
5.12: 92
5.13 (LXX): 92–93
5.24–27: 84
5.31: 94
6: 31–32
6.1–2: 94, 96
6.2–4: 95
6.3: 100–103
6.5: 111, 118
6.7: 118
6.11: 103n27
6.12: 107
6.14–16: 104
6.33: 102–3
6.34: 103
6.35: 104
6.36–40: 33–34, 104–9

7: 30–31, 70
7.2–3: 111–13, 115
7.4: 115
7.5–7: 115–17
7.12: 111, 117–18
7.16: 117
7.19–20: 117
7.19–22: 118

1 Kings
  2.1–10 (1 Sm 2.1–10): 89
  2.12 (1 Sm 2.12): 48
  8–11 (1 Sm 8–11): 73

3 Kings
  9.11 (1 Kgs 9.11): 62

4 Kings
  17.10 (2 Kgs 17.10): 61
  19.35 (2 Kgs 19.35): 69

1 Chronicles
  16.8–36: 89

2 Chronicles
  26–28: 40n10

Judith
  9.7: 113
  13.1–10: 113–14

Job
  3.3: 47
  18.5: 40
  18.5–6: 42–44

Psalms
  2.12 (2.11): 63
  6.7 (6.6): 69
  18.10–11 (19.9–10): 77
  21.23 (22.22): 92
  26.1 (27.1): 113
  26.3 (27.3): 113
  31.9 (32.9): 80
  32.16 (33.16): 111
  38.13 (39.12b): 71
  67.27 (68.26): 109
  71 (72): 106
  71.6 (72.6): 106
  71.7 (72.7): 41–42
  73.19 (74.19): 96
  90.7 (91.7): 72
  91.13 (92.12): 78
  103.15 (104.15): 82
  106.6 (107.6): 62–63
  106.14 (107.14): 62–63
  118.103 (119.103): 77
  118.165 (119.165): 42
  111.9 (112.9): 118
  120.1–2 (121.1–2): 75

Proverbs
  1.20–21: 78
  3.34: 62
  4.23: 96
  8.1–3: 78
  9.3: 78
  9.9: 106
  13.9: 42

Ecclesiastes
  8.5: 49

Song of Songs
  5.3: 108–9

Wisdom of Solomon
  16.20: 49

Sirach
  2.11: 64
  10.12: 62

22.19: 69
25.2: 63

Isaiah
  1–39: 40n10
  1.1: 40n10
  1.4: 63
  6: 40n10
  6.1–3: 40
  9.2–7: 106n42
  11.1: 87
  11.1–9: 106n42
  12.3: 109
  14.12–22: 101n9
  30.2–5: 40n9
  35.3: 116
  36.6: 40n9
  63.1–2: 99

Jeremiah
  2.20: 61
  4.3: 95
  8.23 (9.1): 69
  26.23 (46.23): 111

Ezekiel
  3.20: 96
  4.1–3: 94
  6.15: 110
  24.13: 109
  28.11–19: 101n9

Hosea
  3.4: 105
  8.4: 73
  10.12: 95

Joel
  1.4: 111

Amos
  7.1: 111
  8.11: 73

Haggai
  2.20–23: 101n9

INDEX OF HOLY SCRIPTURE

Zechariah
  3.3–5: 110
  6.12: 101n9

Malachi
  3.20 (4.2): 40–42,
    100n4

New Testament

Matthew
  1.6: 87
  1.20: 87
  3.12: 107
  5.8: 110
  5.14: 46
  5.16: 117–18
  5.19: 116–17
  6.3: 68
  6.4: 60
  6.6: 60
  6.24: 56
  7.13: 69
  7.13–14: 80
  9.18–26: 81
  9.37: 107
  10.23: 115
  10.32–33: 52
  10.38: 112
  11.15: 89
  12.43–45: 60
  12.44: 60
  13.11: 118
  13.22: 95
  16.19: 59
  16.24: 72, 114
  18.10: 85
  22.11–13: 110
  24.12: 46
  24.22: 47
  25.21: 71
  25.33: 68
  25.41: 68

Mark
  4.3–14: 102–3
  4.15: 102–3
  5.21–43: 81
  7.21: 53
  8.34: 112, 114

Luke
  2.13: 64, 68, 87
  8.12: 102–3
  8.40–56: 81
  9.23: 112
  9.62: 72
  12.35: 117
  12.50: 97
  13.27: 68
  13.30: 83
  14.26: 112
  14.27: 112, 114
  14.33: 112–13
  18.8: 46
  21.19: 97

John
  1.9: 39–40, 42,
    44–46
  3.16: 50
  6.28–29: 50
  6.35: 87
  6.51: 87
  10.34–35: 91
  12.31: 98
  13.4–5: 108–9
  13.8: 108
  13.13–14: 109
  14.6: 69
  15.1: 87
  15.3: 108
  17.20: 108

Romans
  1.26: 58
  1.28: 58
  1.28–31: 74
  1.29: 58
  2.5: 61
  2.5–6: 58

  2.12: 100
  4.25: 53
  5.3–4: 97
  7.23: 55
  8.26: 93
  8.38–39: 57
  9.31: 81
  11.2–4: 54–55
  11.5: 54
  11.25–26: 81, 85
  11.30–31: 106
  12.1: 92
  12.19: 114

1 Corinthians
  2.9: 90
  2.14–15: 75, 80,
    82–83, 103, 107
  3.1–2: 82–83, 85, 87
  4.16: 48
  5.5: 59–60
  10.11: 54, 59
  10.18: 95 (Vulgata)
  10.31: 60
  15.26: 84
  15.48–49: 80

2 Corinthians
  2.15: 63
  5.21: 49
  6.14–15: 45
  10.5: 71
  11.14: 42, 44, 107

Galatians
  1.4: 45
  2.20: 51–52
  4.2: 87
  4.29: 75
  5.1: 116

Galatians *(cont.)*
  5.22: 96, 102
  6.8: 95
  6.14: 72

Ephesians
  2.2: 62, 64, 98
  3.10: 80
  3.14–15: 55
  4.27: 67
  5.8: 100n4
  5.16: 40, 45
  6.11: 55, 87
  6.12: 92–93
  6.14: 87
  6.14–17: 114
  6.16: 87–88
  6.17: 87

Philippians
  1.4: 116
  1.21: 51
  2.6–8: 62
  2.10: 55
  3.8: 72, 90

  3.14: 78
  3.17: 48
  4.13: 52, 93

Colossians
  3.1–2: 78
  3.5: 57–58, 83
  3.16: 118

1 Thessalonians
  3.8: 116
  5.8: 87

1 Timothy
  6.20: 43

2 Timothy
  2.3: 113–14, 116–18
  2.8: 53
  3.16: 76

Hebrews
  1.14: 64
  2.12: 92
  4.12: 70
  5.12–6.1: 87

  6.6: 51
  9.11: 99
  11.32–34: 106, 108
  12.12: 116
  12.13: 116

1 Peter
  1.19: 87
  2.5: 92
  2.9: 88
  4.11: 50, 60, 69, 75, 83, 93, 99, 110, 118
  5.5: 62

1 John
  4.1: 107

Revelation
  5.9: 97
  6.9: 98
  6.10: 98
  19.16: 88
  21.8: 115

www.ingramcontent.com/pod-product-compliance
Lightning Source LLC
Chambersburg PA
CBHW020324010526
44107CB00054B/1963